The

# History of Rock 'n' Roll:

The  RHINO
# History of Rock 'n' Roll: the 70s

## ERIC LEFCOWITZ

Byron Preiss Multimedia Company, Inc.
New York

Pocket Books
New York London Toronto Sydney Tokyo Singapore

An Original Publication of POCKET BOOKS

POCKET BOOKS, a division of Simon & Schuster Inc.
1230 Avenue of the Americas, New York, NY 10020

Byron Preiss Multimedia Company, Inc.
24 West 25th Street
New York, New York 10010
The Byron Preiss Multimedia World Wide Web Site Address is: http://www.byronpreiss.com

ISBN 0-671-01175-8

First Pocket Books paperback printing November 1997

10 9 8 7 6 5 4 3 2 1

POCKET and colophon are registered trademarks of Simon & Schuster, Inc.

Senior Editor: Dinah Dunn
Editors: Harold Bronson and Sarah Diamond
Editorial Assistant: Cindy Schwalb
Cover design: Steven Jablonoski
Interior design: Tony Hom and Michael Mendelsohn of MM Design 2000, Inc.

Printed in the U.S.A.

Dedicated to my son Nathan Lefcowitz who loves ABBA.

Author's Special Thanks To:

Harold Bronson and Sarah Diamond at Rhino,
Dinah Dunn and Cindy Schwalb at BPMC,
Duane Dimock, Anita Sethi, Rita Sethi, Bill Inglot, Seth Feinberg,
Meg Handler, Joyce at Cuneiform Records,
Bill Levenson at Polygram, Bob Divney, and Michael Ventura.

# Table of Contents

The **RHINO** History of
Rock 'n' Roll

# INTRODUCTION

The music of the '70s? *Boogie oogie oogie. That's the way, uh-huh, uh-huh. Do a little dance, make a little love. Stayin' alive, stayin' alive.* Not taken seriously? Oh, come on. Next thing, you'll tell us the Pinto wasn't a great car.

Look, the music of the '70s was a lot of things—innovative, uninhibited, silly, rude, off-the-wall, pretentious, offensive, charming, daring, experimental, outrageous, over the top, middle-of-the-road, bloated, excessive, and sometimes just plain strange— but please don't call it serious.

Let's put this in perspective. We're talking '70s here. Baseball players were swapping wives, Patti Hearst was robbing banks, a peanut farmer was running for president. And if that wasn't enough, when you turned on the radio some fool was singing "ooga chaka, ooga chaka."

That was the true '70s experience. So let's get one thing straight from the start. The music of the '70s was only a reflection of society: one moment completely normal, the next moment completely absurd and insane.

And yet, that was part of the fun of being a music fan in the 1970s—the element of surprise. Tuning into Casey Kasem's Top 40 countdown, you might hear Al Green singing "Let's Stay Together," followed by some pop oddity like "Eres Tu (Touch the Wind)" and then "Heartbeat—It's a Lovebeat" by the DeFranco Family.

Unlike the practices of today's music industry, where demographic research is conducted to pinpoint a consumer's desires and where separate channels cater to your individual taste, the 1970s were an era of mass appeal. To be a dedicated music fan, you had to be open to new sounds, and above all, you had to be tolerant.

Listening to your favorite 50,000-watt AM station, you were liable to hear some funky soul ("Lady Marmalade"), some confessional love songs ("You're So Vain"), some uplifting disco ("1 Will Survive"), some dark metal ("Don't Fear the Reaper"), some bubble-gum rock ("I Think I Love You"), and some straight-ahead classic rock ("Takin' Care of Business")—sometimes in the same set.

The key to understanding the music of the '70s is that there was something for everybody. From Barry Manilow to Barry White music consumers could chose from an unprecedented variety of styles and sounds. Punk, funk, techno, reggae, soft rock, hard rock, even rap—the '70s had it all.

It seems sort of ironic, given the diversity of the musical offerings, that for a time, the music of the '70s was considered disposable fluff. But it not only survived that reputation but transcended it. Here are five reasons why:

The RHINO History of Rock 'n' Roll

(1) *The songs are memorable.* The '70s were a golden age of songwriters. Among those who were near or at the top of their craft were Bob Marley, Elvis Costello, Stevie Wonder, Van Morrison, Curtis Mayfield, Joni Mitchell, Carole King, David Bowie, Warren Zevon, Marvin Gaye, Alex Chilton, Lowell George, Randy Newman, Barry White, Donald Fagen, Neil Young, Elton John, Gram Parsons, and (add your favorite here).

(2) *It still sounds contemporary.* Thanks to technology, recording techniques in the '70s improved exponentially. This did not improve music per se, but it did improve the clarity, and clarity matters in a digital age. Also, technological advances provided more options for musicians, thus contributing to the overall variety of sounds.

(3) *It seems larger-than-life.* In the pre-video era, the rock concert reigned supreme. Creating a spectacle became an essential ingredient in maintaining a festive atmosphere. The big shows included Parliament's "Mothership," Pink Floyd's inflatable pig, Kiss's blood-spitting pyrotechnics, Alice Cooper's snakes and guillotines, and Elton John's piano-pounding theatrics. Rock was never bigger or more outrageous.

(4) *It invites participation.* From the Village People singing "Y.M.C.A." to the audience participation rituals of *The Rocky Horror Picture Show*, the ethic of the '70s was to get people involved in the festivities. This was particularly true in disco. As the group Chic sang on "Good Times," "Don't be a drag, participate."

(5) *And last, but not least, it had a sense of humor.* One of the reasons the music of the '70s remains fresh is because of its irreverence. In the late '60s, music took a serious turn. In the '70s, it lightened up, returned to its roots, and became party music. And just when it was threatening to become self-parody, along came the punk rockers to give the music scene a swift boot to its swelled head. That was funny, too.

Together—songcraft, technology, theatrics, participation, and humor—it adds up to a pretty impressive legacy. But really, there is no reason to argue whether the music of '70s is worthy of a revival—it's already happened. And that is why it is so important to put the current '70s revival in its proper place. We must be vigilant in our effort to make sure we do not lose touch with what made the decade so memorable, so diverse, and occasionally, so mortifying. Seen your high school yearbook picture recently? OK, then, case closed.

If we are going to be honest about it, then we should admit we are enjoying the '70s from a safe distance, secure in our hazy recollections about all of those jaw-dropping lapses of taste. And maybe that's a good thing. Now that all of the emotional roadblocks have been removed, there has never been a better time to enjoy the music. You can love the Ramones *and* Gary Glitter *and* Queen *and* the Village People—in fact, you can hear their songs played during time-outs in sports arenas.

Listen to "Get Down Tonight" by KC and the Sunshine Band. It is a perfect example of how the passage of time has reshaped our memories. In 1975, when the song first came out, the rock cognoscenti sneered; and yet, now, over twenty years later, it has new cachet. Why? Because it's carefree, it has a good beat, and it reminds us of our ninth grade dance party.

Does it matter whether "Get Down Tonight" is a rock classic? Of course not. In the end, discussing the integrity of the music of the '70s is like analyzing episodes of "Charlie's Angels" for signs of subliminal feminist messages. It's fun, sure, but it's really just another intellectual exercise.

One of the reasons the sounds of the '70s continue to endure is the songs were interwoven into the fabric of the times. Like short bursts of history, each one captures a split-second nuance or emotion. Throughout this book, we have attempted to string

together these brief snapshots in time to tell the story of what it was like to be a music fan in the 1970s.

That is why we prefer to call this book an interpretative history of the '70s rather than a literal one; after all, no one hears the same music the same way. And, likewise, no two people would write the history of '70s music the same way as well.

It is nearly impossible to sum up the history of the music of the '70s in one linear story. Instead, we have attempted to focus on specific themes of the decade's music scene and shed a little light on the performers and movements which characterized the era.

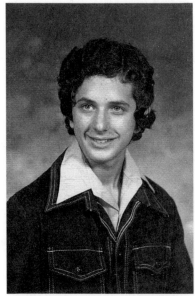

*Eric Lefcowitz: Yearbook Photo, 1977*

One thing you will not find in this book is sordid tales of backstage intrigue. Also missing are the time-worn stories behind the big hits of pop, rock, and soul of the 1970s. We also won't bore you by recounting and recalling the same old facts and figures, the ones we've read about time and time again.

Also, it should be noted that this book does not attempt to cover every single artist of the decade. Some music—actually, quite a lot of music—has fallen through the cracks, music which helped define the '70s: the reggae sounds of Bob Marley and the Wailers; the new wave pop of the Knack and Devo; the soft rock of James Taylor and Carole King; the experimental rock of Brian Eno and Wire; the musical genius that was Hamilton, Joe Franks, and Reynolds (just wanted to see if you're paying attention).

Plus, there were all those great singles: Gladys Knight and the Pips' "Midnight Train to Georgia," Albert Hammond's "It Never Rains in Southern California," T-Rex's "Bang a Gong (Get it On)," Dobie Gray's "Drift Away," and Rod Stewart's "Maggie May"—all of them wonderful records. It just so happens they do not fit into the purview of the essays contained in this book.

Of course, that means a lot of vital music is missing. But, the intention of this book is not to be an encyclopedia—there are many fine examples out there for the choosing—the intention is to provide some context on the musical movements of a complex decade.

The history of the '70s is far too complex to sum up in a few words. There are too many one-way streets and dead ends. Historical context is lost in the flow of images lodged in our collective memory. Jim Jones—click—reminds us of Kool-Aid—click—which reminds us of TV commercials—click—which reminds us of Mikey, the kid who'll eat anything.

Jim Jones to Mikey. That's what you're up against if you are trying to capture an entire decade of music in one book. But that is also what makes the subject of the '70s so endlessly fascinating. Between 1970 and 1979, a mind-boggling agglomeration of songs wedged their way into our pop consciousness. And, over twenty years later, they continue to bring pleasure to old and new listeners alike.

A typical '70s pop song? If there was such a thing, it managed to reflect the mood of the times yet remained constantly upbeat and insidiously catchy. Like Sammy Davis Jr. singing about "groovy lemon pies" in "The Candy Man"—it was silly, it was cool, and it was shamelessly escapist. Perhaps in the final analysis, this is the greatest asset of music of the 1970s: the sound of people trying to have a nice day.

—Eric Lefcowitz,
New York City, 1997

# HAPPY DAYS

*"Come on, get happy."* – "The Partridge Family" theme song, 1972-75

In a decade full of unforeseen trends, one of the biggest surprises of the 1970s was the renewed interest in the 1950s. This phenomenon saw movies such as *Grease* and *American Graffiti* become box-office hits, TV shows like "Happy Days" dominate the Nielsen ratings, and rock 'n' roll revival shows tour to capacity crowds.

It was almost as if the '60s had never happened. Almost. Of course, in reality, the '60s had just happened—which probably explains the sudden fascination with all things '50s. After the race riots and all of the turmoil surrounding the Vietnam War, the relatively innocent '50s reminded people of the good old days.

Never mind the McCarthy witch-hunts and the Communist menace—those were aberrations. The '50s were a time of white picket fences, tail-finned Thunderbird convertibles, drive-in movie theaters, and unlocked doors—not to mention, unlimited prosperity.

*Hello sunshine, goodbye rain: Happy Days*

That image of a vital, strong America brimming with post-war pride and confidence was fondly recalled, even by people who weren't born in the '50s. After all of the division and anguish of the '60s, a culture of reconciliation was needed, and looking back, the '50s seemed to suit those needs to a tee.

Returning to the '50s, musically, meant returning to a sunnier age when rock music was played at sock hops, when Elvis had a smaller pelvis, when groups called themselves the Crew Cuts and the Monotones and sang uncomplicated songs like "The Book of Love." It meant returning to a time, as Archie Bunker sang, "when girls were girls and men were men."

There were no paisley-wearing, psychedelic, long-haired dandies in the '50s and none of that freaky acid-rock music either. And for that reason alone, the '50s were mighty appealing. Hot rods and drag racing and "rebels" like James Dean were light years away from the darkness which had descended over the country in the late '60s.

Much to the dismay of people who enjoyed good-time rock 'n' roll, the music of the '60s had also turned dark and foreboding. The feedback wailing of Jimi Hendrix on "The Star-Spangled Banner," the brooding, atmospheric rock of The Doors and the Velvet Underground, the spiky protest songs of Jefferson Airplane—each was an echo of the inner turmoil that had been tearing the country apart.

That sense of loss and regret was still evident on the *Billboard* pop charts as the '70s began. Songs about coming to terms with pain and struggle such as Simon and Garfunkel's "Bridge Over Troubled Water," the Beatles' "Let It Be," and Marvin Gaye's "What's Going On" spoke of troubled times in the culture at large.

A new trend was visible, however, a decidedly more happy phase. It first reared its sunny head in late 1969, when "Na Na Hey Hey Kiss Him Goodbye" became a number-one smash for the group Steam.

That song's preternaturally-upbeat sentiment—which in many ways, foreshadowed disco—was a way of saying goodbye to the sadness of the '60s and hello to a brave new world of the '70s. Its chorus was a demon-exorcising chant which promised a fresh start, a clean break with the past, a new beginning.

After the agonizing years of conflict, a weary society seemed willing to put aside its differences and paint a cheery gloss over ugly reality for the sake of getting along. The symbol that came to represent this act of reconciliation was the omnipresent icon of the "happy face."

The happy face was ubiquitous in the early 1970s. It was impossible to escape its beaming presence. Everywhere you turned, a yellow face with the cheek-to-cheek grin was smiling down at you from magazine covers, clocks, notebooks, bumper stickers, buttons, and T-shirts. It was a perfect representation of a peculiar moment in history. In a conscious attempt to remain upbeat, to throw off the solemnity of the past and celebrate life, people from all backgrounds decided, en masse, to embrace an image of perpetual bliss (not surprisingly, some interpreted the happy face's beatific grin as the bleary-eyed gaze of someone who was surreptitiously stoned).

A whole happy-face culture emerged. There were happy-face communes, happy-face cults, and a happy-face organization of well-scrubbed youth called Up With People. As a reaction to the gloom and doom in the world, people had gone completely . . . happy.

The musical offshoot was the flowering of upbeat happy songs, songs with good vibrations. After all, rock music wasn't just darkness—it was also about having a good time. "I Just Want to Celebrate" by Rare Earth and "Joy to the World" by Three Dog Night were indicative of this new trend, one which continued building toward the giddy excesses of disco.

### The Top 10 Singles of 1970

1. "Bridge Over Troubled Water"-Simon and Garfunkel
2. "American Woman"-Guess Who
3. "Get Ready"-Rare Earth
4. "Band of Gold"-Freda Payne
5. "Raindrops Keep Fallin' On My Head"-B. J. Thomas
6. "ABC"-The Jackson 5
7. "Let It Be"-The Beatles
8. "Close To You"-Carpenters
9. "Mama Told Me Not To Come"-Three Dog Night
10. "War"-Edwin Starr

The ebullience of a line like "joy to the fishies in the deep, blue sea" was, lyrically and spiritually, about as far away from "say you want a revolution" as one could imagine. But after a decade of divisiveness, ebullience was in demand.

If celebration had been missing in music, it could now be found in abundance. Happy-face songs began flooding the marketplace in the early '70s. Number-one hits included Tony Orlando and Dawn's "Knock Three Times," The Osmonds' "One Bad Apple," Ray Steven's "Everything is Beautiful," Sammy Davis Jr.'s "The Candy Man," Johnny Nash's "I Can See Clearly Now," and Maureen McGovern's "The Morning After."

Carefree and lacking even the slightest hint of political commentary, the happy-face phenomenon was a dramatic about-face for pop music. Lengthy acid-rock jams and indulgent concept records had previously been considered de rigueur in established rock circles. The buzz among cognoscenti was "progressive rock," a fusion of technology like Moog synthesizers with the foundations and melodic complexity of classical music.

Happy-face music lacked those ambitions. Instead, it took its cues from the original rock 'n' roll of the '50s. What made the original rock 'n' roll so invigorating—and so worthy of resurrecting—was its simplicity and, of course, its innocence.

The desire to return to more innocent times and, by association, more innocent music, explains the emergence of groups such as the Carpenters ("Close to You"), Climax ("Precious and Few"), and Bread ("Make It With You") in the early '70s. Although criticized as bland and middle-of-the-road, they, in fact, reflected the state of the union and market demand.

The public had made its choice. Instead of the raw emotions and politically charged sentiments of '60s rockers, they wanted the untroubled, carefree, cruising music of Chuck Berry, Jerry Lee Lewis, Roy Orbison, Gene Vincent, Ricky Nelson, and Frankie Lymon.

"The day the music died," according to songwriter Don McLean, was the day in 1959 when Buddy Holly, one of the original rockers of the '50s, was killed in a plane crash. It was Holly's demise that served as the central metaphor for McLean's 1971 smash "American Pie"—a seven-minute kaleidoscopic journey through pop culture.

Like no other song of its era, "American Pie" managed to capture the mood and tone of that fascinating, and slightly odd, transitional period between the 1960s and the 1970s when people were attempting to recapture their lost innocence and, at the same time, move forward.

Music, as always, played an essential role in chronicling the changes, but more than ever, its role was ambiguous. "Do you believe in rock 'n' roll," McLean sang early in the song, "can music save your mortal soul?"

In a nutshell, this became the crucial question regarding music in the '70s. Could music change the world, as the artists of the '60s had suggested? Or was it merely a good excuse to "rock 'n' roll all night and party every day," as Kiss would sing?

*Don McLean*

"American Pie" offered no easy answers. But it did testify to the power of the music. By weaving so many allusions to rock stars into the song, McLean underscored the way that rock music had become an essential device in tracking the progress of our lives. It also spoke of our need and desire to believe in heroes.

More than ever, rock fans wanted something they could relate to, something exciting, something they could surrender to so thoroughly and completely that they would lose hold of their senses. In a sense, they wanted a "new Beatles"—not the bickering long-haired Beatles of the late '60s, but those cheerful, clean-cut Liverpool lads who sang songs about holding hands on "The Ed Sullivan Show."

In retrospect, it seems almost preordained that the Beatles would cease to exist as a unit in the 1970s. They were, after all, synonymous with the '60s. Had they stayed together, the music scene of the '70s undoubtedly would have been different. But how different . . . who knows? It's like wondering what would have happened if Hitler had gotten into art school. He didn't.

*The dream is over.*

You couldn't change reality. The Beatles had broken up. As John Lennon announced on his album *Plastic Ono Band*, the dream was over. But people didn't want to accept that fact—for one thing, it was a downer. And in the happy-face culture, there was no room for downers. So people just kept on searching for the excitement of a full-blown mania like the Beatles and finally they got it—disco! Of course, few would have linked the rise of disco to the Beatles (disco was the anti-Beatles in detractors' minds), but through the Bee Gees, a connection to the "fab four" unquestionably existed.

As early as the mid-1960s, the Gibb brothers had been tagged "the next Beatles." They finally broke through in 1978, when a series of upbeat songs from the mega-selling *Saturday Night Fever* soundtrack made the Bee Gees superstars. When the trio placed three singles from that album in *Billboard's* Top Ten, it matched a record set by the Beatles themselves.

But the Bee Gees' meteoric rise was a curious one. What explains the phenomenal sales and public attention? What did the brothers Gibb offer the public besides catchy dance music and quivering falsetto harmonies? Perhaps it was simply the idea of brotherhood and fraternal unity. After all, the Beatles unity, in a very real sense, had always been their strength. Through their seemingly unshakable faith in each other, there was an unspoken promise that people's efforts, when united, could create something greater than the sum of their parts.

And, yet, by engaging in a highly public and acrimonious split, the Beatles had provided the '70s with a stark lesson about what happens when such dreams fall apart, so theirs was a cautionary tale.

The Bee Gees resurrected the myth of the Beatles without any of the social significance, thus, they were a perfect representation of the '70s. Ironically, their only

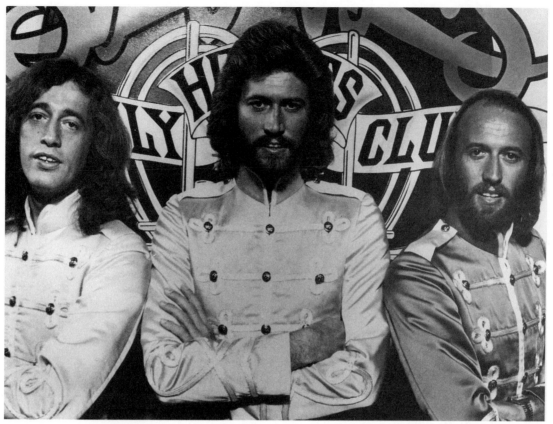

*Robin, Barry, and Maurice Gibb*

misstep was to star in the movie version of the Beatles' *Sgt. Pepper's Lonely Hearts Club Band.*

To the surprise of no one, *Sgt. Pepper*, the movie, was a box-office disaster. It was a useful disaster, however, because it meant, finally, gratefully, that the obsession with finding the next Beatles had come to an end. From now on, any "next Beatles" sightings either fell into the category of a hoax or a simulacrum. Phony Beatlemania had bitten the dust.

But in many ways pop was never the same. After disco, the classic three-minute pop single became a vanishing species. Its implicit promise—eternal youth—did not correspond with the demographics of an aging population. Ex-hippies were becoming proto-yuppies. The market for catchy, three-minute singles was drying up, replaced by teenagers seeking new sensations.

The death of the Beatles-styled pop hit in the '70s opened the door for two anti-pop phenomena: one based on dance beats and sex (disco) and another based on martial drums and alienation (punk).

At the same time as those movements were taking hold, the old war-horses of the '60s—Bob Dylan, the Rolling Stones, the ex-Beatles—carried on as if nothing had happened. Despite the nagging sense that their best years were behind them, they kept touring and releasing albums.

Toning down the revolutionary rhetoric of the past, the heroes of the '60s counterculture gravitated, musically, toward introspection. For example, Jefferson Airplane had encouraged listeners to "feed your head" in the '60s; in the '70s, the newly-christened Jefferson Starship sang ballads whose operative philosophy was "if only you believe in miracles."

The curious notion of the '60s that music would change the world was replaced in the '70s by a new sentiment: music was entertainment and rock performers were the entertainers. Mick Jagger, perhaps unconsciously, echoed that point in a song called "It's Only Rock 'n' Roll (But I Like It)."

The Rolling Stones were emblematic of the dilemma that '60s rock stars faced in the '70s. They were millionaires with every earthly pleasure available at their command, and yet, they were expected to maintain their integrity; i.e., not sell out to "the man."

Like Jefferson Starship, the Stones saw the writing on the wall and toned down their "fighting in the streets" rhetoric in favor of making good-time party music like "Happy." Even after their double-album masterpiece *Exile on Main Street*, when the Stones' members and music grew increasingly dissolute, Jagger and company managed to hold on to their mythic status.

* * * * * * *

## Words of the '70s

*People have this obsession: They want you to be like you were in 1969. They want you to, because otherwise their youth goes with you, you know.*

—Mick Jagger

* * * * * * *

Many of their contemporaries were not as lucky. Ironically enough, the heroes of the '60s were struggling with the same problems the original rockers touring in those '50s revival shows had once faced: how to stay relevant in a new era.

"Don't trust anyone over thirty." That was the anti-establishment maxim of the 1960s, and many performers were pigeon-holed in that era. As they approached that dreaded age of thirty, trouble loomed. Many, facing the prospect of growing old in rock 'n' roll, just opted out altogether—as witnessed by the untimely deaths of the perpetually 27-years-old Jimi Hendrix (1970), Janis Joplin (1970), and Jim Morrison (1971).

"Hope I die before I get too old." That wonderfully brash line in the Who's anthem "My Generation" was coming back to haunt the self-styled revolutionaries of the '60s (but not The Who's Keith Moon who, to no one's surprise, made good on its promise in 1978).

Rock was made for the young—that was the cruel lesson. And the concerns of rock's biggest market, teenagers, were considerably different from superstar musicians with chalets in the south of France. But how do you sing about the problems of the common man when you are living a jet-set lifestyle and rich beyond belief?

You don't—and this may explain why bands like Kiss and Grand Funk Railroad rose to prominence in the '70s. They made a calculated pitch to working-class kids who didn't ask for "Silly Love Songs," but expected "Revolution."

A few artists emerged who managed to weld a '60s sensibility to their introspective songs and make vital music in the process. Artists such as Jackson Browne, Joni Mitchell and the Eagles, all of them consummate '70s performers, were, in many ways, more closely linked to the spirit of the '60s.

Mitchell wrote "Woodstock," which presaged the "got-to-get-back-to-the-garden" ethos that many of her '60s brethren were only too happy to indulge in. But she, unlike many of her contemporaries, was willing to change styles and push boundaries on jazz-inflected albums like *Blue* and *Court and Spark*.

Jackson Browne

Jackson Browne had seen the counterculture up close in the hippie enclaves that were scattered throughout Topanga and Laurel Canyons, in California. Over the span of several records, he reflected back on that bygone spirit to great effect, concocting elegies to the diminished dreams of the '60s in songs such as "Before the Deluge," "Running on Empty," and "The Pretender."

And the Eagles, beneath that sunny California rock exterior, were always redolent with edgy despair. The songwriting team of Don Henley and Glenn Frey cleverly masked their odes to crushed ideals with beautiful three-piece harmonies. But there was a dark underbelly to their best efforts: "Desperado," "Lyin' Eyes," and particularly "Hotel California," whose cynical kiss-off to the lethargy of the '70s was the bitter riposte: "We haven't seen that spirit here since 1969."

That spirit did seem to be missing in action. Only a few of the old protest guard, like George Harrison, who put together "The Concert for Bangladesh," or Bob

*Who the hell are these guys? President Ford meets George Harrison, Billy Preston, and Ravi Shankar.*

Dylan, who joined him and later spoke up for former boxer and convicted murderer Rubin Carter on the song "Hurricane," seemed willing to put their politics on the line.

The musical journey of Dylan, in particular, was emblematic of the challenges facing '60s rock stars in the '70s. First he went small and country, then he went big and massive with Rolling Thunder Revue, then he went underground with the release of *The Basement Tapes*. Finally he ended up a born-again Christian on *Slow Train Coming*.

# Words of the '70s

*Just because you like my stuff
doesn't mean I owe you anything.*
—Bob Dylan

Bob Dylan—
jamming for Jesus

The irony of that earnest '60s folkie crooning "Blowing In the Wind" becoming a Christian proselytizer demanding you "Gotta Serve Somebody" was perhaps the ultimate representation of how much things had changed in the course of a decade.

But if Dylan's aberrant behavior spoke volumes about the confusion of the '70s, it also showed how former revolutionaries were having a hard time remaining au courant. Former folksinger Phil Ochs apparently was so aggrieved at the changes he saw around him that he ended up taking his life. Idealism had its limits.

The writing was on the wall when Sonny and Cher, the apostles of the hippie culture's happy face, decided to split up. Already the Beatles had broken up, the Stones were stoned, and Dylan was preaching the gospel.

Who was minding the store? Or, more importantly, who was singing about the issues of the day like James Brown did on "Funky Watergate (People It's Bad)"?

The only rock group, apparently, that was willing to take on Watergate was Lynyrd Skynyrd, a band whose attitude and music were about as far from the idealistic '60s as possible. "Watergate doesn't bother me," Ronnie Van Zandt sang smartly on "Sweet Home Alabama," "Does your conscience bother you?"

This ended up being one of the most piquant commentaries on a Top 40 hit in the 1970s, because it dealt with the one issue that happy music tried desperately to gloss over: that people had differences of opinion. It wasn't just black or white, happy or unhappy—there were shades of gray.

By embracing the '50s, the trend setters in pop culture were making a conscious attempt to steer away from moral complexities. There was the unspoken hope and belief that the unrest and division of the '60s had only been just a blip on the radar screen.

One way that people tried to come to terms with the 1960s was simply to avoid the conflicts of the era. An example was the sudden popularity of lava lamps and bean bags. When these silly but harmless fads became fixtures in America's living rooms in the 1970s, it was symbolic of how society had changed since the turbulent days of the prior decade. Lava lamps were remnants of 1960s psychedelia—something you could gaze at for hours, especially if you were zonked out on some illicit substance. And bean bags were an alternative mode of relaxation, places to "crash."

In a subtle sense, by allowing lava lamps and bean bags in their homes, many parents were consciously avoiding the kind of "love it or leave it" battles that had characterized the generational wars of the '60s. If it took accepting some relatively

* * * * * * *

# Words of the '70s

*As far as any rock 'n' roll revival thing is concerned, I don't really freak about the '50s. I mean, I love Elvis and I remember going to see Bill Haley when he came to Britain— they were so visual in their tartan suits and all . . . but I also like singers like Billie Holiday and Frank Sinatra. I think we're updated rather than just '50s. As far as my hair is concerned, well—there are just so many ways you can wear your hair, and obviously, everything is going to remind you of something.*

—Brian Eno of Roxy Music, *Creem,* May 1973

* * * * * * *

benign ephemera of the 1960s flower-power culture to avoid conflict—well, many thought, so be it.

A culture of acceptance and reconciliation was the hallmark in those first years of the '70s. This was true in politics as well as music. When Ray Stevens had a number one hit with "Everything is Beautiful" in 1970, the sentiment may have seemed corny and cloying but after years of social unrest, racial division, and the Vietnam War, it was, in its own modest way, a breakthrough.

But then came the overkill. There were so many messages of togetherness that, after a while, they were all rendered meaningless. A case and point was "I'd Like to Teach the World To Sing," a song made famous in 1972 Coca-Cola commercial.

"I'd Like To Teach the World to Sing" was a perfect distillation of the happy-face culture. The very simple idea behind the song—a hit for both the Hillside Singers and the New Seekers—was that if you could gather enough people on a hillside, break open some Cokes and sing this song, everything would be beautiful (in its own way).

In retrospect, the sudden efflorescence of upbeat pop in the early '70s had reached its peak. The culture of despair and death which had torn apart the country in the '60s had been replaced by the sound of John Denver's singing "Thank God I'm A Country Boy." Like any movement, there were limits—you could be *too* happy. As Denver proved, sometimes happy face music could be oppressively upbeat. Odes to joy like "Me and You and a Dog Named Boo" and "You Light Up My Life" could make you woozy with their saccharine and sappy sentiments.

A backlash was inevitable. There was only so much "Sunshine on My Shoulders" ("makes me happy") and "Summer Breeze" ("makes me feel fine") that rock fans would take. After all, it is the nature of rock 'n' roll to shock.

*The good old days.*

Since the mid-'50s—when pioneers such as Elvis Presley, Gene Vincent, and Jerry Lee Lewis upset the staid Eisenhower era with unabashed sexuality and pounding drum beats—rock music has been a constant source for new sensations.

But of course, as we now know, the '70s were really anything but innocent. The indelible image of the "me decade" is and will always be the debauchery of the slogan "sex, drugs, and rock 'n' roll." That's why the non-offensive, melodic pop that you can still hear today while getting your hair cut or waiting on the telephone for a customer service representative (a.k.a., "lite rock") is not really indicative of the classic '70s sound, even if it came out of the '70s.

Ultimately, the real lesson of happy-face music was that you couldn't go back—not to the sock hop, not to the soda fountain, and most of all, not back to innocence. Ricky Nelson, '50s teen idol, realized the limits of nostalgia when he claimed, on his 1972 hit "Garden Party," that if memories were all he had to offer, he'd "rather drive a truck."

Perhaps, in the final analysis, the fractured and fractious music scene of the '70s can be seen as a search for the specter of unity the Beatles had lent the '60s. The Beatles made happy music, sad music, heavy music, light music, funny music—sometimes all on the same album. But John Lennon had been right. The dream was over. In the '70s, people were only unified in their need to escape.

It just so happens the last number-one *Billboard* hit of the 1970s was also called "Escape (The Piña Colada Song)." But the last hit of the '70s bore no resemblance to the desultory mood of ten years before. It was downright cheery.

# GIMME GIMME SHOCK TREATMENT

*"Leary of the waltz/mash-potato schmaltz" –"Do the Strand," Roxy Music, 1973*

Rolling over shards of glass, leaping wildly into the audience, and generally acting like a madman, Iggy Pop was the physical embodiment of "shock rock" in the early 1970s. He provided the spark that lit the fuse that resulted in the punk rock explosion later in the decade.

On their seminal 1970 album, *Fun House*, Iggy and his band, the Stooges, made dark and demon-possessed music that gave voice to the legions of listeners who felt alienated from the social and political climate of the '70s.

There was something unholy—even threatening—about the way Iggy shouted "I feel alright" on the song "1970." It was a full frontal assault on the feel-good, mellow rock that was dominating the *Billboard* charts at the time, which was exactly the point. Shock rock turned the happy face of the '70s upside down and revealed the truth about everyday life. Sometimes, like the sound of the Stooges, it was ugly.

*Iggy Pop: "Everyone has a shadow and I like to project a big one."*

The musical chops of the Stooges may have been questionable at best, but the blunt force of Iggy's delivery and the sonic ferocity of his aggressively amateurish bandmates provided an adrenaline rush light-years ahead of its time.

Embracing dischord and ignoring commercial acceptance, Iggy and the Stooges created music that redefined the boundaries of rock rebellion. And by doing so, they laid down the gauntlet for every shock-rock band to follow: Alice Cooper, the New York Dolls, Kiss, the Ramones, Patti Smith, the Dictators, Talking Heads, Richard Hell, the Sex Pistols, the Damned, the Clash, the Germs, and the Buzzcocks.

Shock rock was everything that happy hippie music was not. Where the latter sought harmony, the former embraced disharmony; where the latter represented unity and order; the former gave voice to chaos and disorder.

The music of Iggy and the Stooges embraced the wretchedness of existence, the baleful and noxious fumes of industry, the odious machinations of culture, the abominable excess of Western society, and by doing so, exorcised some of its oppressive power.

Most people missed the point. Iggy's antics were infamous, but they were also unwelcome. His crude and primal approach was sheer effrontery to proper middle-class American mores. And to make matters worse, the Stooges were all but rejected by the rock community as well.

Why? Because Iggy's scandalous behavior was a stain on the happy-face culture of the '70s—a slap in the face of the Woodstock dream. They had the nerve to sing about bad vibrations.

Unlike the sunny songs of California rock like the Eagles ("Take It Easy") and sensitive songwriters like Cat Stevens ("Peace Train"), Iggy and the Stooges ("Search and Destroy") gave off the whiff of danger, of primal drumbeats being played in dank clubs filled with disreputable people.

Iggy's corrosive presence on the rock scene of the early 1970s was virtually ignored by mainstream audiences—hardly a surprise considering his penchant for self-lacerating behavior. Although both *Fun House* and its equally amazing follow-up *Raw Power* were to remain cornerstones of shock rock, it wasn't until the mid-to-late '70s punk explosion in New York and London that the protean rage of their music was given its full expression, not to mention its full due.

But in between the inevitable commercial demise of various incarnations of the Stooges and the rise of punk rock, a watered-down, but tremendously successful, version of shock rock came out of the clubs to storm the commercial world of arena rock.

The performer who brought the shock rock of Iggy Pop to the masses was Vincent Damon Furnier, a.k.a., Alice Cooper. He and his eponymously named band were linked by stylistic association with the no-holds-barred theatrics of Iggy and the Stooges. But the comparison ended there. The difference between Cooper and the Stooges? Many, many millions of dollars.

Cooper, the man and the band, took shock rock to the top of the charts, aided by a pair of terrific singles—"School's Out" and "Eighteen." Both were perfect summations of teen alienation, spit-ball rebellion, and inarticulate frustration. But what separated Alice Cooper was not the music—it was a mind-blowing stage show.

*Half a boy and half a man—Alice Cooper shocks the masses.*

The chicken incident. It appears to be the key to understanding the Coop. . . . It was years ago in Toronto that Alice, during one semi-inspired piece of improvisation, chased a live chicken around the stage.

"I held the chicken out to the audience and threw it up in the air, expecting it to soar. Instead it did a nose dive. Suddenly the kids were pulling it apart. The next thing I heard in the press was that I had bitten its head off and sucked its blood."

"Now I ask you," says Coop, waving at the row of golf clubs and petting the puppy more vigorously than usual, "would I do that? I mean—*honestly*. Alice wouldn't even *think* of doing that."

— *"Creature Feature" by Steven Rubenstein,*
Circus Magazine, *August 24, 1976*

As a concert attraction, the Alice Cooper show became an urban legend. Snakes unfurled, dolls were dismembered, blood spurted, and guillotines chopped. It was fun, fun, fun, 'til Daddy took the Uzi away.

Cooper's elaborate "Grand Guignol" stage show circa 1971 would probably seem quaint, maybe even hokey by today's standards. And that makes sense. After all, the point of all great shock rock is to shake things up in the present, not the future, when it is bound to appear old and stale.

Cooper injected excitement back into the rock experience. Just when clichés threatened to turn the spontaneous concert ritual into a predictable set of moves— flashpots and power chords, T-shirts on the main concourse, a haze of smoke wafting through the stadium—Cooper transformed it into something electric again.

But Cooper's stage show was in many ways just an act—in real life, he was a perfectly conventional and patriotic citizen. He copped to voting Republican and playing golf in exclusive clubs—if it wasn't for the excessive sex and boozing, he could have remained a lifetime panelist on *Hollywood Squares.*

Inevitably the fans of shock rock, in their insatiable quest for more titillation, moved on to greater thrills, and the half-life of Alice Cooper ended after a few years of upsetting the establishment. Officially, Alice was "over" to the shock-rock audience when he scored a massive hit record with the ballad "Only Woman" in 1975.

The successors in arena shock rock was Kiss. Their first hit single in 1975, "Rock and Roll All Nite," was a crucial addition to the beer-drinking, doobie-smoking, brain-cell-depleting, SAT-score lowering frat-rock classics of the '70s.

Like much of the shock rock of the '70s, everything about Kiss was a finely calculated marketing plan—from the misspelling of "Nite" (naughty, naughty) to the borrowed Nazi imagery of the lightening-bolt stylized "SS" in the Kiss logo. The kabuki-style make-up, the pyrotechnics, the smoke, the hydraulic drum risers, the flashpots, the killer light show—it was all designed to grab people by their lapels and not let go.

Was any of it real? Well, let's put it this way—Gene Simmons (a.k.a., Gene Klein) later admitted in interviews that he had given serious thought to becoming a rabbi. But, on second thought, he decided to become a rock star who wagged his tongue and spit out blood. Nice work if you could get it.

It was no surprise that Kiss was hated and loved in equal measure. But the band's impact on the decade cannot be underestimated. Blockbuster tours, mega-selling albums, comic books, movies, lunch pails, make-up kits, 3-D Viewmaster reels, pin-ball machines—Kiss was a true multimedia band. And their fans, the so-called Kiss Army were loyal to their real-life, blood-vomiting, cartoonish rock stars: Simmons, Paul Stanley, Ace Frelay, and Peter Criss.

## Words of the '70s

*I guess I've always wanted to be God. What that really means really is that I was to be It. Mr. Cool. Mr. Top. And there's nothing higher than God. I don't know if I want the responsibility of knowing that all the atoms in the universe are going all right. But it would be great to have your name repeated all the time—'Thou art great, Thou art this, Thou art that.' Yeah, I sure am.*

"Blood on the Wax, The Kiss Tapes, Part IV: Gene Simmons"
*Circus Magazine*, July 22, 1976.

Critics argued that Kiss was just four anonymous performers playing anonymous heavy metal. But there are just as many people who will tell you Kiss changed their lives—or at least shocked them out of their suburban idyll. Unlike the mainstream rock of, say, Foghat or Bad Company, Kiss offered its fans an escapist fantasy which spared no frills.

But Kiss also had a half-life. When Cher left Sonny Bono and was seen cavorting with Simmons, Kiss had clearly gone Hollywood. Every time a shock-rock act went mainstream—how else can you describe the band's power-ballad "Beth"?— the world of rock was due for another sensation. And it just so happens the next sensation was a good deal rawer and, for that matter, more shocking.

Enter punk rock—the Ramones, the Sex Pistols, the Clash, Generation X, the Germs, the Dead Kennedys, the Avengers, the Dead Boys, Johnny Thunders and the Heartbreakers, X-Ray Spex, the Buzzcocks, and all of the other dyed-hair, ripped T-shirt, safety-pin-through-the-nose, expletive-un-deleted bearers of bad news, bad vibes, and bad-ass attitudes.

What fun . . . and what a relief. When punk reared its ugly head in the mid-1970s, the buzzards were just beginning to swirl around the bloated carcass of the "dinosaurs of rock"—the huge arena rock bands who made up for the lack of excitement onstage by offering audiences laser-light shows, extended drum solos, and huge sound systems.

Fortunately, the great thing about rock music is that every time it threatens to anesthetize its audience with some hokey form of showbiz theatrics, someone is waiting in the wings to storm the stage and slay the dragons of predictability. In 1976, that person was Johnny Rotten.

Perhaps too much has been written about punk rising out of nowhere, sui generis. The truth is the Sex Pistols were about as spontaneous as the Bay City Rollers. After manager Malcolm McLaren had a close-up look at sleaze-rock masters the New York Dolls, he knew where the bread would be buttered. Taking his cue from the Dolls, McLaren cooked up a ploy to shock the masses for the sake of making an art statement.

But to give McLaren his due, the masses needed something shocking. And to give the Sex Pistols their due, they made an extraordinary noise. The sight of a sneering, enraged Rotten spitting out "I am an anti-Christ" was just the jolt needed to energize moribund rock audiences stoned on ludes and lulled to sleep by the gentle, three-piece harmonies of Poco.

*The Sex Pistols*

Whether the Pistols were calculated or spontaneous, the group's incandescent 1977 debut album, *Never Mind the Bollocks, Here's the Sex Pistols,* was a milestone of shock rock. Virtually all of the band's finest moments were captured on one slab of vinyl: "Anarchy in the U.K.," "God Save the Queen," "No Feelings," "Pretty Vacant," and "EMI."

With its roaring guitars and Rotten's vituperative lyrics oozing attitude, *Never Mind the Bollocks* was and is a sonic blueprint for aspiring punk rockers. It has proven so influential that many people are under the mistaken impression that punk rock began and ended with the Sex Pistols.

But in truth, the Sex Pistols were just another addition to a long line of shock rockers. If anything, the mantle of punk rock could just as easily rest on the shoulders of the Ramones, the New York-based quartet whose "Blitzkrieg Bop"— a perfect summation of the group's trademark chainsaw-buzz guitar sound— opened their debut album in 1976.

*Ramones* reads like a rock 'n' roll reactionary's manifesto. The kind of driven, primal, mind-blasting r&r that fueled the Stooges fanclubs and formed the editorial backbone of fanzines from *Who Put the Bop* to *Punk* comes alive in "Blitzkreig Bop," "I Wanna Be Your Boyfriend," and "Chainsaw." . . . Serving its radical function, the Ramones' debut drives a sharp wedge between the stale ends of a contemporary music scene bloated with graying superstars and overripe for takeover. Right now, Ramones have their hands on the wheel.

—*Ramones review by Gene Sculatti,* Creem, *vol. 8, #3, August 1976.*

*"For me it was like I was an old car and I was being taken out for a ride at one hundred miles per hour; and I kinda liked it, because I was really getting rid of a lot of rust." —Norman Mailer, on attending a Ramones concert*

Although the Ramones were too inarticulate to spell out the alienation and disenfranchisement that gave rise to their thunderous brand of music—and the scene gathering at New York clubs like CBGBs and Max's Kansas City—the group told you all you needed to know with three simple chords and song titles like "Now I Want To Sniff Some Glue."

1-2-3-4! From Dee Dee's countdowns to Joey's fabulously gawky stage appearance, the Ramones stripped the excess from rock 'n' roll and created a shockwave that rippled across the Atlantic.

If the Ramones were the foundation of the second wave of '70s shock rock, it took the Patti Smith Group to lend the shock-rock movement a poetic edge and art-school credentials. "Jesus died for somebody's sins but not mine," Smith sang in the first line of her classic 1975 album *Horses*. At the end of her titanic live reading of "My Generation," recorded in 1976, Smith threw down the gauntlet for every garage band catching whiff of the New York scene: "We created it, let's take it over."

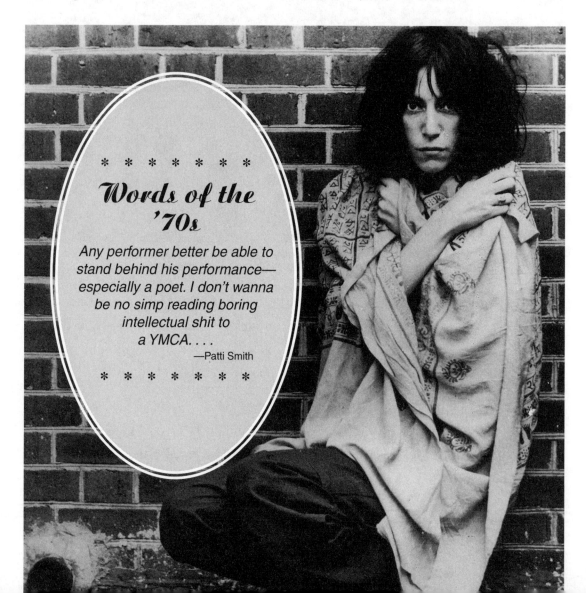

* * * * * * * *

## *Words of the '70s*

*Any performer better be able to stand behind his performance—especially a poet. I don't wanna be no simp reading boring intellectual shit to a YMCA. . . .*

—Patti Smith

* * * * * * * *

The shock-rock bands that were coalescing around New York were a community of like-minded individuals who shared a do-it-yourself ethic—one that encouraged others to pick up guitars and give it a try, including bands such as Blondie, Talking Heads, the Dictators, Television, and Richard Hell and the Voidoids.

Unlike the larger-than-life theatrics of Alice Cooper and Kiss, the latest incarnation of shock rock invited the participation of its audience. One of its essential contributions was breaking down the walls between the audience and the performer.

When Richard Hell tore his T-shirt, it was truly an act of rebellion. The rock T-shirt had become the ultimate totem of '70s arena rock, something to be worn until it was faded. But as Hell sang on "Blank Generation," he could "take it or leave it anytime."

A similar do-it-yourself aesthetic was evident in movies like *Pink Flamingos* and *The Rocky Horror Picture Show*. The former, directed by John Waters, used "found actors" and real locations in Baltimore. This wickedly

*Divine(above) and Tim Curry—*
*Sweet transvestites from transexual Transylvania.*

tasteless comedy, created on a minuscule budget, managed to push the boundaries of good taste and become an underground independent cinema hit at the same time.

*The Rocky Horror Picture Show* was a different breed altogether—a taboo-busting rock musical with all of the Hollywood trappings. The camp classic, which starred Tim Curry and Susan Sarandon, was ruled a box-office bust until a cult following, based on midnight screenings, created its own phenomenon.

But the true link between *Rocky Horror* and the denizens of shock rock wasn't Meat Loaf or its Roger Corman-esque mock-horror sensationalism, it was the rite of audience participation—dressing up as characters, throwing objects, and yelling back lines at the screen. Like shock rock, *Rocky Horror* was designed to evoke a response, and by evoking it, managed not only to knock down that wall between itself and its audience, but also transform the event into a spectacle of its own.

The New York punk scene—and all of the mini-punk rock scenes it fostered in San Francisco, Akron, Los Angeles, and London—stressed community over material success. And tacitly, they encouraged the end of hero worship. "No more heroes anymore," sang the Stranglers in 1977 and they meant it.

The last thing rock needed in the '70s was another untouchable icon. The lasers swirling around Jimmy Page as he noodled endlessly on his guitar made him out to be someone with gifts beyond the mere mortal. "Clapton is God," went the famous graffiti. But shock rock revealed we were all merely mortals—a healthier approach but also heretical to those who mistook rock for religion.

That is why shock rock was often misunderstood. It wasn't about who had the biggest bulge in his jeans or whose box-office receipts had the greatest skimming

potential—it was a revival of the spirit of making music for the love of it, and if it exposed a few hypocrisies along the way, so be it.

Exponents of shock rock like the Sex Pistols took the concept of individual liberty and pushed the possibilities to the extreme. Sid Vicious was the new breed—the fan who became rock star. He was the genie in the bottle McLaren had envisioned when he invented the Sex Pistols. It was the shocking notion that you—yes, you—could pick up a guitar, even if you couldn't play it, and join a band, just like Vicious.

But, of course, there was nothing really new about that idea. The torso of Iggy Pop— "the world's forgotten boy"—had long since healed when Vicious decided to rip open his flesh with broken bottles and bleed all over his bass. But Vicious, by his mere presence, spoke of new possibilities. Self-invention was a crucial part of shock-rock lineage. Creating and maintaining a unique character was essential—particularly if that character was disreputable in one fashion or another.

"There's a new sensation/A fabulous creation," Bryan Ferry sang in the opening lines of Roxy Music's 1973 single, "Do The Strand." For all purposes, Ferry could have been singing about himself. He and Roxy Music, although rarely given credit, were role models for a cerebral approach to shock rock.

\* \* \* \* \* \* \*

# *Words of the '70s*

*I don't have any rock 'n' roll heroes, they're all useless.*
*The Stones and The Who don't mean anything anymore,*
*they're established. The Stones are more like a business than a band.*
—Johnny Rotten

\* \* \* \* \* \* \*

What was shocking about Roxy Music? It was the shock of the new. Ferry's odd bursts of falsetto, the atmospheric sax of Andy Mackay, and the dramatic tension between the guitar heroics of Phil Manzanera and the powerful drumming of Paul Thompson, combined to create a sound that was a radical departure from the 4/4 beat of their glam rock peers.

Roxy's stage attire, like its music, pushed the envelope of what was acceptable on the rock stage—gold lamé troubadour suits, silver boots, and dyed hair were par for the course. But there was a good deal of humor behind these antics. Ferry's decadent lounge singer was an acute commentary on rock star clichés, and by flaunting them all, he helped demystify them in the same instant.

Another progenitor of shock rock through humor was Frank Zappa. If James Brown was the godfather of soul, then Zappa was the godfather of shock. His twisted parodies of hippie culture (*We're Only in It for the Money*) with the Mothers of Invention were milestones of satire in the '60s. But Zappa put his highly idiosyncratic stamp on the '70s as well with albums like *Weasels Ripped My Flesh, Apostrophe,* and *Over-Nite Sensation.*

# Words of the '70s

*Historically, musicians have felt real hurt if the audience expressed displeasure with their performance. They apologized and tried to make people love them. We didn't do that. We told the audience to get fucked.*
—Frank Zappa

* * * * * * *

Zappa had an ineffable love for offending people's sensibilities. He embraced subjects like sexual perversion and rock groupies with gusto. To his credit, he also lent his largesse and reputation to various artists through his label Straight, most significantly the early recordings of Captain Beefheart and Alice Cooper.

And while we're on the subject of shock-rock originators, what about Lou Reed, whose '60s outfit the Velvet Underground practically invented the form? As a solo artist in the '70s, Reed made a few crucial contributions, including his 1975 double-album *Metal Machine Music*. Four album sides of screeching feed-back—if that wasn't shocking, what was?

Lou Reed

But Reed's 1972 album, *Transformer*, did provide a crystalline moment of '70s underground vérité with "Walk on the Wild Side," a surprise Top 40 hit that was notable for slipping the phrase "giving head" on to AM radio. The album, one of Reed's most successful, was produced by the ubiquitous David Bowie, a prototypical glam rocker himself.

Bowie was deeply intertwined with the history of '70s shock rock. As a self-styled shock-rock hero, he played a mentoring role model to the less successful Reed, as well as Iggy Pop and Ian Hunter. He even got John Lennon some action with "Fame."

*"I was an instant star; just add water and stir."*
*—David Bowie*

In 1972, Bowie's androgynous, make-up wearing, sexually ambiguous creation Ziggy Stardust became a seminal shock-rock pose. Years before Kiss applied a pancake base, Bowie had perfected the role of rock star icon. But Bowie's theatrical voice gave it away—he was playing a role of shock rocker.

Throughout the '70s, Bowie released a terrific series of singles, including "Changes," "Rebel Rebel," "Young American," "Golden Years," "Fame," and "Heroes." As a testament to his ever-shifting wardrobe of styles, each song sounded different.

Like any good actor, Bowie had impeccable fashion sense. He heard Iggy and then made it Ziggy. He took the shock value of androgyny and then chucked it when it became useless. He went decadent blue-eyed soul (i.e., his Thin White Duke phase) and then disappeared. When he re-emerged, he had transformed the surreal ambience and offbeat nuances of German bands like Tangerine Dream and Kraftwerk and created the albums *Low* and *Heroes.*

As Bowie discovered, the right uniform made you a shock rocker. But by doing so, he exposed a flaw—given all of the right accoutrements almost anybody could buy into the club. Take, for example, Reg Dwight—a pudgy, balding, gap-toothed performer who, on first glance, seemed like anything but pop star material. And yet, when he donned an outrageous pair of glasses—presto!—he became Elton John, a piano-pumping showman tour de force.

It didn't matter that Elton John made sublime pop music. To compete in the market-place of shock-rock antics he needed to transform himself into a cross-dressing Jerry Lee Lewis who sang tough-boy songs like "Bitch Is Back" and "Saturday Night's Alright for Fighting."

Despite the theatrics, Elton was always "shock-rock lite." There was nothing really shocking about his career, except his bisexuality, which only became a full-blown controversy when Elton outed himself in the late '70s; otherwise, musically, he was as safe as milk ("Philadelphia Freedom" was practically the American Bicentennial anthem).

Elvis Costello faced the same dilemma. If there was a drawback—a credibility gap—to shock rock of the 1970s, it was that talented musicians like Declan MacManus had to become Elvis Costello if they hoped to break through to a larger audience. MacManus was a crooner at heart, but onstage as Costello he became a twitchy stage persona to attract attention.

The shock-rock moves employed by Costello overshadowed the fact that he, like Elton John, was one of the most gifted songwriters of the '70s. Eventually, the good Elvis won

*Elvis Costello*

out. The transformation was complete when he took Nick Lowe's "(What's So Funny 'Bout) Peace, Love, and Understanding" and, without the slightest hint of irony, gave it a sincere reading.

But sincerity had little to do with shock rock. In the end, outrage was its measuring stick. And after a while, like any fashion, when the stick became shtick, the potency of the message began to wane. When the Rolling Stones, in an misbegotten attempt to maintain their fading shock-rock credentials, ran an advertisement for their 1975 album *Black and Blue* featuring a picture of a bruised woman who was bound, gagged, and smiling (a snafu which resulted in a boycott of Warner Communications by feminist groups), it was a sign of things to come.

Inevitably, the one-upmanship mentality began to rob shock rock of some of its charm. When Kiss added their blood to the red ink used by Marvel Comics to make a comic book, was it shocking or just exploitative? That question would come more into focus in the early '80s when everybody and his Twisted Sister started jumping into the shock-rock game.

In the final analysis, what set apart the shock rockers of worth from the poseurs was humor—a wink and a nod that came across in those perfect three-minute songs like "Oh, Bondage, Up Yours!" (X-Ray Spex) and "Orgasm Addict" (The Buzzcocks). Humor transcended the self-mocking, archly ironic, and sometimes sleazy antics that the times required.

When shock rock first began to slither up the cultural totem pole in the early 1970s, it was considered a threat to the decency and the morals of the nation. By making unholy racket with a "heart full of napalm," Iggy and the Stooges were explicitly rejecting the then-prevailing trends in music that placed a premium on getting in touch with and self-actualizing your inner self.

But you didn't have to be a dyed-in-the-wool cynic or a nihilist to question the sincerity of so-called enlightened souls who addressed the world's problems with finger cymbals and flowers. Although shock rock, rather than happy-face culture, took the blame for many of society's problems—teen suicides, drug abuse, the breakdown of morality—to its credit, it never traded its wares on the false promise of transcendence.

It couldn't whiten your teeth or improve your sex life, but the music of shock rock was authentically a voice of liberation. Its main achievement was to shake the populace out of its mass somnolence. By acknowledging the dark side, glamorizing decadence, popularizing nihilism, flaunting sexuality, and encouraging anarchy, the performers of shock rock provided a necessary antidote to the gooey excess of a sappy and sentimental culture as seen and heard on TV and radio. And by making sure to offend everyone, shock rock guaranteed it would not be forgotten.

The Dead Kennedys keeping the hardcore spirit alive.

# THE REVOLUTION WILL NOT BE PLAYLISTED

*"I don't care what the people may say, I don't give a ***** anyway."*
—Mott the Hoople, "Death May Be Your Santa Claus," 1972

Peter Frampton had pin up good looks. Ian Hunter did not. Frampton was one of the most successful performers of the '70s. Hunter had one hit single and then disappeared from the rock scene.

The radically different fortunes of Peter Frampton and Ian Hunter were, in many ways, symbolic of the music industry as a whole in the 1970s. Some people struck it rich, others just faded away—sometimes for reasons that seemed utterly random.

Frampton and Hunter were not as dissimilar in real life as their dramatically different fortunes would lead one to believe. Both were English, both began new bands in 1969—the former joined Humble Pie, the latter joined Mott the Hoople—and both favored a basic hard-rock guitar approach.

But the rock gods move in mysterious ways. Just when Hunter was enjoying a career-saving hit with David Bowie's "All the Young Dudes" in 1972, Frampton decided to leave Humble Pie and seek fame and fortune on his own. And here's where the story splits off into two wildly disparate paths.

Mott the Hoople are a pack from Britain who have learned Bob Dylan's classic period in much the same way that Badfinger learned the Beatles. Their first album contained the finest and most letter-perfect cops from *Blonde on Blonde* and floating tapes of that era since Procol Harum's debut, but Mott cut Procol by not only rendering Dylan with as much finesse, maybe even a little too much more than the master showed at his best moments, but also by revealing a sense of humor that he would have appreciated.

— *Brain Capers' review,* Creem, *vol. 3, #11, April 1972*

*"Let's face it, I'm a showoff." —Peter Frampton*

*Ian Hunter*

In 1976, the same year Hunter broke up Mott the Hoople, Frampton stunned the musical world by selling twelve million copies of *Frampton Comes Alive!* What happened? To this day, no rational explanation has ever been provided. It was just one of those perfect moments in pop music when everything converges at exactly the right moment. The year Frampton came alive—1976—was the year of the American Bicentennial celebration, and his brand of non-offensive pop-rock was exactly what the people wanted. His timing was impeccable.

Hunter, it turns out, had less impeccable timing. After Mott the Hoople broke up (its guitarist, Mick Ralphs, went on to found the enormously successful Bad Company), Hunter was essentially a washed-up rocker at the age of 30, one whose relentless partying had already landed him in the hospital.

Why would Peter Frampton, so close to stardom after a decade, release a live, double-record set when he really hasn't established a large audience? He says, "I just wanted to do an album that summed up the first four solo records in the most effective way possible." . . . *Frampton Comes Alive!* is more than a summation of his solo career; it's also a synthesis of the best third-generation British rock styles. As the genre's brightest light, it will be interesting to see where he takes it from here.

—*Review of* Frampton Comes Alive! *by Jean-Charles Costa,*
Rolling Stone, *March 11, 1976*

Was Hunter's fate undeserving? Or for that matter, was Frampton's fate undeserving? It is impossible to make such judgments. Just as you can't judge a record's merits by its sales, you can't proclaim its brilliance because of its lack of sales.

And yet, facts are facts. The bigger the rock business became in the '70s the more it was predicated on albums like *Frampton Comes Alive!* and *Boston* and Fleetwood Mac's *Rumours* and the Eagles' *Hotel California* and the soundtrack to *Saturday Night Fever.* These were the blockbuster albums of the 1970s—the ones that changed the mentality of the music business.

If an album like Frampton's could sell twelve million copies, the logic went, then why bother with some obscure, raw talent. Find more Framptons! The flaw of this logic, of course, was that it ignored all of the impassioned but less-commercial artists whose innovations would eventually change the course of music.

Talent needs to be nurtured. But as the '70s progressed, the odds were stacked against musicians who took chances and experimented with form. Their reward was not money or fame, it was integrity, purity, and, just as often, obscurity. This was the music that didn't shift millions of units or become classic rock, yet it was just as worthy and fulfulling.

All you had to do was substitute Hunter's name for Frampton's ("Hunter Comes Alive!") or plug in John Prine for Bruce Springsteen, Alex Chilton for Elton John, Iggy Pop for Alice Cooper, Nils Lofgren for Bob Seger, Faust for Genesis, or NRBQ for Grand Funk Railroad.

There was a whole class of artists whose careers could be summed up by one dreaded term: one-hit wonders. One of the most famous one-hit wonders of the '70s—and an instructive example of how commerce and art make uneasy bedfellows—is Neil Young.

Although Young had been on the music scene in bands such as Buffalo Springfield and Crosby, Stills, Nash & Young, the Canadian-born singer with the high-pitched warble was an unlikely prospect of having any kind of hit before his single "Heart of Gold" became a surprise chart-topper in 1972.

Neil Young

As it turns out, "Heart of Gold" would also be his last commercial hit. Dissatisfied by the middle of the road, Young "headed for the ditch," as he later wrote in the liner notes to the compilation *Decade*. "A rougher ride," he added, "but I saw more people there."

Indeed there were plenty of people there, particulary struggling musicians. Thanks to the vagaries of the record business and the rise of FM radio, a recording act had to have an identifiable hit song. That was the hidden truth behind the popular and dominant '70s radio format known as album-oriented rock (AOR).

AOR had been modeled on an underground radio format which emerged in the late '60s where DJs were allowed to set the mood. This encouraged impromptu and

*The Top 10 Singles of 1972*

1. "American Pie- Parts I & II" - Don McLean
2. "Alone Again (Naturally)"- Gilbert O'Sullivan
3. "Without You" - Nilsson
4. "Brand New Key" - Melanie
5. "I Gotcha"- Joe Tex

6. "Daddy Don't You Walk So Fast" - Wayne Newton
7. "Let's Stay Together" - Al Green
8. "The First Time Ever I Saw Your Face" - Roberta Flack
9. "Brandy" - Looking Glass
10. "Lean On Me" - Bill Withers

experimental sets of music where there were no rules—i.e., no playlists. But AOR brought back playlists. It was an unwritten but undeniable reality: radio stations using the AOR format employed a playlist of hit album tracks.

A hit album track was different than a hit single. First of all, it did not have to be a staple of AM radio or crack the hallowed *Billboard* Top 40. In fact, it did not even have to be a single. The greatest "hit" in the history of the AOR format, "Stairway to Heaven," was never released as a single but still received enormous airplay.

The logic was obvious: AOR hits sold albums, and albums made more money than singles. But the drawback was equally obvious: By encouraging the creation of hit songs, less challenging music was going to come to the fore. Anything that seemed too intellectual or abrasive (or for that matter, funky or soulful) was rejected in favor of the straight-ahead rock approach of Bachman-Turner Overdrive's "Takin' Care of Business," an AOR staple.

This was "classic rock," a highly restricted club of a few dozen acts who dominated the music scene of the 1970s. One of the inevitable by-products of their massive success was to deny access to artists who couldn't find a signature hit on that phantom AOR list and thus were doomed to labor in obscurity.

Neil Young was a notable exception. Despite his success in the AOR format with albums such as *Harvest* and *After the Gold Rush*, Young refused to remain complacent and continuously challenged the formula of hit-oriented rock. Instead of making palatable mainstream rock, he revealed an explicitly uncommercial sound that favored meandering, unpolished songs which embraced a variety of downbeat emotions.

This decision to opt out of the star-making machinery resulted in a spectacular set of albums—*On the Beach, Zuma* and *Tonight's the Night*. On *Tonight*, Young grappled

*Tom Waits—Not in heavy AOR rotation*

with the recent overdose deaths of band-mate Danny Whitten and friend Bruce Berry. These emotionally threadbare albums, for a time, virtually destroyed Young's commercial potential but as he cleverly noted on his 1979 comeback record *Rust Never Sleeps*, "it's better to burn out than it is to rust."

Young's "fallow" period was all-but-undocumented on radio. For all intents and purposes, he just disappeared. The same story applied to many innovative musicians. Unless you could pick up a college radio station, the chances that you would hear the New York Dolls and Tom Waits and Can in the same set were slim-to-none, despite the fact that all of them were making ground-breaking music at the time.

FM radio, as Donald Fagen wisely cracked, meant "no static at all." He knew the game. Along with his Steely Dan collaborator Walter Becker, Fagen continually managed to skirt the limits of what the heavily playlisted format would allow. By throwing in jazz timings, disjointed lyrics, and an overtly intellectual approach to making rock, Steely Dan excelled where most failed. Even though, as a band, they hardly ever toured or made public appearances, they still received plenty of airplay and, therefore, sold healthy amounts of records.

The majority of recording acts, however, suffered a drastically different fate—no airplay, constant touring, and meager sales. This is often the fate of less-commercial musicians. Respected by fellow musicians but ignored by the public, incredibly influential on future generations but virtually unheard in their own time, these are the artists who are accorded cult status, a title almost as dreaded as one-hit wonders.

The '70s, like any decade, boasted dozens of artists who developed these cult followings and not much else. This allowed them to tour and, if lucky, keep making records; if they were content with their fate, they could keep making uncompromised music that touched the lives of a small but devoted audience.

Jonathan Richman is a textbook example of an unheard '70s artist. His influence cannot be measured by million-selling records or packed stadium concerts, but Richman and his band, the Modern Lovers, contributed a unique presence on the underground rock scene of the 1970s—and, for a time, they were truly underground. The group's original 1972 recordings, including the classic "Roadrunner," remained unreleased until 1975. By that time, the band had already broken up.

Two of the members of the Modern Lovers eventually went on to bigger things—drummer David Robinson ended up with the techno-pop band the Cars and keyboardist Jerry Harrison joined Talking Heads. But Richman chose the path not taken, traveling from town to town with his acoustic guitar, singing songs of

Velvets meets Stooges meets Doors meets boy next door . . . who has this sinus condition.

—*The Modern Lovers review,*
Creem, *vol. 8, #3, August 1976*

Jonathan Richman

childlike wonder such as "Ice Cream Man," "Dodge Veg-O-Matic," and "I'm a Little Dinosaur"—songs that guaranteed a limited cult audience.

Richman's unabashed innocence and quirky boy-next-door charisma made for an arresting stage presence. But what chance did his seriously silly songs have in the hallowed halls of corporate rock where the bottom line remained record sales and gross receipts? Apparently, judging from his modest earnings, not much. The name Jonathan Richman meant next to nothing in the '70s—at least compared with names like Clive Davis or David Geffen, presidents of record divisions, who perversely became celebrities themselves.

The '70s was a golden era for record industry moguls. Robert Stigwood had the hottest run. In late 1977 and early 1978, his RSO Records had six straight number-one singles that spent twenty-one weeks at the top of the charts thanks, in large measure, to the spectacular success of the Bee Gees.

And then there was Casablanca Records and its charismatic president Neil Bogart, who sold box loads of Donna Summer and the Village People. He was the man who green-lighted the plan to release four solo records by the members of Kiss simultaneously (amazingly, all four records went platinum).

But impresarios like Stigwood and Bogart did not establish themselves by following their hearts and their ears; they became rich and famous by consistently landing the big ones—the mega-selling, stadium-filling acts. They were always on the lookout for the latest craze (Get more Framptons!) and took pride in duking it out in frenzied bidding wars to land the act that had created the biggest buzz.

Such is the case with the "new Dylans." Ever since Bob Dylan had emerged in the early '60s and revolutionized the world of rock, talent scouts had been scouring clubs on the lookout for the next harmonica-and-guitar songwriting genius with a penchant for clever lyrics and good put-downs. Neil Young had once been touted as a "new Dylan" in the '60s.

But in the '70s the expectations were raised when Dylan seemed, for a time, to be slipping out of the mode that made him popular. The time was right, certain labels thought, for a real "new Dylan." As a result, several artists, including John Prine, Townes Van Zandt, Louden Wainwright III, and Bruce Springsteen, were handed prestigious recording contracts.

Of course, a letdown was inevitable. How could anybody be a "new Dylan?" But the case histories of Prine, Van Zandt, Wainwright, and Springsteen offered a fascinating study of what it was like to live up to the hype generated by their various record company publicity departments and, conversely, dealing with the disappointment of diminishing returns.

To link John Prine and Bob Dylan took no extraordinary stretch of imagination; Prine's folksy drawl was bound to invite the comparison. Like Dylan, Prine used a spare compositional style and had a painter's eye for detail. His topics often drifted toward unobserved subjects—Vietnam veterans, old folks, and, in general, to dreams deferred. "Paradise," an ode to his roots in Kentucky, was a typically evocative look at lost landscapes of forgotten small towns.

Like many of the "new Dylans," Prine leavened the dark despair of his music with bursts of levity and generous amounts of self-deprecating humor. Although greatly appreciated within his own ranks (Prine received the highest honor that any "new Dylan" could be accorded when the old Dylan joined him onstage and sang his songs), he still struggled to make a living in music.

John Prine

Despite the accolades for his classic 1971 debut album, *John Prine*, and subsequent releases such as *Sweet Revenge*, Prine strained, in parlance of the trade, to "shift units." That was no surprise, really. Prine's candid portraits, stripped of pretension in a marketplace that encouraged pretension, had a hard time being heard.

Like the other "new Dylans" it was only a matter of time before Prine would find himself without a recording contract or the support of a major label. The situation had been prophetically summed up by Dylan himself many years earlier when he wrote, "how does it feel/to be on your own/with no direction home/a complete unknown/like a rolling stone?"

Townes Van Zandt, one imagines, would have had an interesting answer to that question. He, too, had been anointed a "new Dylan" and, undoubtedly, read the press accounts calling him a genius. But it seemed Van Zandt wanted little, if not nothing, to do with the Faustian bargain of being the new anything. He made that clear on the 1971 release, *Hi, Low and in Between*, an album filled with wry observances that embraced the outsider mentality to perfection.

On the song "No Deal," Van Zandt likened the prospect of imminent success to the insidious come-ons of a car salesman pushing an engineless car. "You don't need no engine to go downhill," the salesman cracks as "he handed me the keys." The metaphor, it seemed, was no fantasy. For Van Zandt the keys were personal demons and the habits he acquired from living life on the edge.

"No Deal" seemed to acknowledge and accept his fate: "I come through this life a-stumblin'/my friends I expect to die that way/It could be 20 years from now or could be most any day." And only a little behind schedule, in 1997, he did. For his fans, the sadness of his slow decline was mitigated by the songs he left behind, including "Poncho & Lefty"—an enormously affecting tale of two drifters cast off from society.

*Louden Wainwright III*

Naked and exposed, full of remorse and longing, Van Zandt was a gentle but restless soul, a honky-tonk angel lost in the wilderness, who lived out the lives of his characters. But Van Zandt did not ask for pity. As he sang on "Poncho & Lefty," "that's the way it goes."

A better fate awaited Louden Wainwright III. He survived, occasionally thrived, and when his "new Dylan" hype died down, displayed crucial survival instincts by finding work as an actor ("M.A.S.H."), scoring a freak hit ("Dead Skunk in the Middle of the Road"), and emerged from the '70s with his integrity, if not his psyche, intact.

Wainwright was no less uncompromising than Prine and Van Zandt. He could fire off a poison-pen love letter like "Old Friend" and deliberately engage in shocking language ("Rufus is a Tit Man") and, some might say, act blatantly insensitive. But that was his charm. His songs captured offhand moments in a demented America, and while hardly a consistent hit-maker, Wainwright continued to record to acclaim into the 1990s.

I saw rock 'n' roll's future and its name is Bruce Springsteen.

*—Future Springsteen producer and manager, Jon Landau,* The Real Paper *May 22, 1974*

Prine, Van Zant, and Wainwright had differing degrees of success. In a way, their careers are more interesting compared to each other than Dylan himself. They all ran on the same folk circuit, struggled with career ambitions, wrestled demons, and were revered and admired by fellow musicians.

Although Bruce Springsteen shared many of the experiences of the "new Dylans," his career arc was different. Two less-than-successful albums—*Greetings from Asbury Park, N.J.* and *The Wild, the Innocent, and the E Street Shuffle*—were suitably Dylanesque to invite comparisons, but thereafter, "The Boss" took a more mainstream approach, writing self-conscious rock anthems and delivering a solid rock 'n' roll punch onstage.

When he dropped some of the Dylan mannerisms and veered more toward straight-ahead rock on *Born to Run* in 1975, Springsteen landed himself the ultimate "thanks, I needed that" prize for an inspiring "new Dylan"—the covers of both *Time* and *Newsweek*. Through perseverance, Springsteen coped with the hype and continued to score platinum after platinum album, peaking with his multi-platinum *Born in the U.S.A.* in 1984.

Not bad for a "new Dylan." And somehow it seemed appropriate—even inevitable—that the arc of Springsteen's career would bring him back to the stark folkie style heard on his stripped-down *Nebraska* and other similarly styled albums. Having gone to the mountaintop, it seemed Springsteen was slowly climbing down, going back, as it were, to being a "new Dylan."

Thankfully the entire phenomenon came to a humorous conclusion when Louden Wainwright III recorded "Talking New Bob Dylan" in 1992. The semi-autobiographical tale, written on the occasion of Dylan's 50th birthday, was sung directly to Dylan himself. With his trademark wryly observant style, Wainwright recalls winning a Bob

*Bonnie Raitt*

Dylan imitation contest and deciding to attempt a career in music. "So I got some boots, a harmonic rack, a D-21, and I was on the right track," Wainwright sings, until he realizes that "being the new you was a helluva job."

For a time, Dylan himself was struggling to be the "old Dylan." There were murmurs in the early '70s that the great one had lost his edge, murmurs that were put at least temporarily to rest when he released the masterful *Blood on the Tracks* in 1975. On "Buckets of Rain," the album's closing track, Dylan provided a little self-help advice to struggling musicians about the importance of following your muse. "You do what you must do," he sang, "and you do it well."

Some musicians were fortunate enough to do it well and hang in there long enough to reap the rewards of their toil. Many artists survived by touring, including Bonnie Raitt. The daughter of John Raitt, the Broadway star of *The Pajama Game* and *Carousel*, Raitt was a prodigal talent drawn to the slide guitar of the Mississippi Delta blues artists.

Raitt's second album, *Give It Up,* was a supremely accomplished effort, an intoxicating mix of Delta shuffles, Dixieland jazz, and confessional singer/songwriter songs like "Love Has No Pride" and Raitt's own shimmering "Nothing Seems To Matter." Dedicated to "the people of North Vietnam" and recorded with the cream of Woodstock musicians, the 1972 album was not a great hit, taking nearly twenty years to go gold. But after long years of struggling, success finally came to Raitt in 1989 with her celebrated album *Nick of Time.*

For every Raitt, whose success was a long time coming, there was an Alex Chilton, who recorded "The Letter," a 1967 number-one smash for the Box Tops, when he was a teenager. After he went solo, Chilton's commercial prospects sank like a stone; however, he kept churning out challenging pop. For a moment, as a member of the much-beloved Big Star, he seemed poised for true rock superstardom, a contender for title of the "next Beatles."

Yes, like the "new Dylans," there were a group of pop bands who were expected to be "next Beatles." After the Fab Four split in 1970, there was a widespread search in the record industry for a group that could replicate their melodic pop sensibility and their sales figures.

The vacuum created by the Beatles' absence allowed plenty of worthy contenders to come to the fore. Post-Beatles pop included the likes of Elton John, Billy Joel, Badfinger, the Raspberries, 10cc, the Knack, Cheap Trick, the Flamin' Groovies, Todd Rundgren, ABBA, and the Electric Light Orchestra.

Most were fine talents with a penchant for knocking out memorable three-minute pop ditties, but ultimately, none had the mystique to go with the musicianship. One of the best and influential of the "next Beatles" was Big Star whose eponymous debut and second record *Radio City* were chock full of tuneful Beatles-fla-vored pop songs like "Thirteen" and "September Gurls." But approximately 316 people bought Big Star's records and, needless to say, the band didn't make the cover of *Rolling Stone.*

Why didn't Big Star live up to its name? Perhaps the music was too idiosyncratic and eccentric or maybe the timing was just off. Often the outcome of record sales hinged on promotion. If a record label didn't see a single that could crack the Top 40, regardless of the disc's quality, the album was doomed for discount bins.

Recalcitrant rock critics have since recognized that Big Star was perhaps *the* great overlooked pop band of the '70s. Some even argue its first two records, in terms of pop values, measured up to anything a solo Beatle released in the '70s. Too bad the band's co-founder Chris Bell, who died in a car crash in 1979, didn't live long enough to enjoy the band's rediscovery.

Still, if you took all of the "new Dylans" and all of the "next Beatles" (we won't even go into the "wannabe Stones") and combined the obstacles they faced in getting their music heard, it didn't come anywhere close to the experience faced by experi-mental bands like Faust and Can.

Although these and other so-called "Krautrock" bands are now considered relevant and highly influential, at the time, their music was truly unheard—at least to the ears of American rock fans. Rock from Germany? That was an unlikely proposition consid-ering there was already enough competition in the U.S. rock market from Canadian and English bands.

But this was not ordinary rock. In fact, it was a complete departure from the world of mainstream sensibilities. While everybody else was using the studio to achieve

sonic perfection and get rid of the random in the '70s, Faust and Can reveled in free-form musical interchange, ambient sound texture, and surprise moments in the studio.

The social and political backdrop to these unearthly sounds played an essential role in their creation. Krautrock arose from a German youth movement which was coming to terms with some of the worst atrocities in the history of mankind. One result of their enlightenment, both chemical and otherwise, was a willingness to accept no boundaries in making music.

Faust was perhaps the most radical exponent of this esthetic. The shifting sound-scapes of their self-titled 1971 debut album made brilliant use of the collage effect, including feedback, tape manipulation, and other sonic irregularities. Onstage, Faust was also known to use industrial power tools to shattering effect. Sometimes a band member would mosey over to a pinball machine and the resultant plinks and bells would weave themselves into the sound texture. It was, to say the least, a distinctly non-commercial approach to making music.

Can also forged a radical departure in music. Although they were more closely rooted in a classical rock style, there was still an air of planned spontaneity to their best work. In particular, Jaki Liebezeit's drumming lent the group's odd-meter rock compositions a mesmerizing drone, the trance-like effect which later surfaced in the spacey electronica of Tangerine Dream's *Phaedrus* and the robotic synthesizer stylings of Kraftwerk's *Man-Machine*.

German bands, on the whole, fared poorly on American radio, although Kraftwerk did have a Top 40 fluke hit in 1975 with "Autobahn." By and large, they were ignored and that was a shame—rock fans missed some of the most adventurous music experiments or any decade.

*Joy Division borrowed Can's dark recesses and Teutonic backbeat.*

But these bands left their mark in other ways. Can, for example, was a direct influence on Joy Division, another revolutionary band of the '70s, who borrowed Can's Teutonic backbeat and mined many of the same dark and moody recesses in their music.

Although their influence outweighed their immediate impact, the members of groups such as Can and Faust, like any innovative artists, were forced to face the ongoing dilemma of musicians who could barely subsist on the money they made. Could they survive and carry on, content with limited success, or would they find the results of their efforts too unrewarding to keep their careers going?

These are the kind of questions that every lesser-known musician has to face at one time or another. Which was the better path to happiness—a commercial or non-commercial approach? And, of course there is no adequate answer. Whether, for example, Peter Frampton's music will outlive Ian Hunter's or vice-versa remains to be seen.

Ironically, Frampton is now considered a textbook example of fleeting fame. His career declined as fast as it ascended. Hunter, on the other hand, is still highly regarded for his efforts to achieve a few precious moments of rock 'n' roll transcendence. Together, they symbolize the mixed blessings of being a cog in the machine of the music business. A success like Frampton might win gold records, but a semi-success like Hunter might win hearts. Which was the better road?

# ONE NATION UNDER A GROOVE

*"Tell all the folks in Russia and China, too."* –The O'Jays, "Love Train," 1975

One of the most perplexing names of a band in the 1970s was the Los Angeles-based outfit War. Although the name conjured up visions of a group that made angry protest music, War was best known for good-time party tunes like "The Cisco Kid," "Low Rider," and "Why Can't We Be Friends?"—all top-five hits in the mid-1970s.

Exactly what category of music did War make? For lack of a better term, you could call it unity music. It was music that conveyed a message of racial harmony and brotherly love—a message that War, as an integrated band, was well positioned to get across.

Employing a whole grab bag of musical styles—a little soul, a little funk, a little jazz, and some Latin rhythms—War made music that knew no boundaries of race or skin color. The laid-back feeling of "Why Can't We Be Friends?" offered a wonderfully seductive vision of a world where people were unified in song. "The color of your skin don't matter to me," the lyrics insisted, "as long as we can live in harmony."

*War! Good God, y'all.*

Could music and songs that explicitly endorsed a spirit of solidarity and tolerance be an effective force for unity between the races, or would music ultimately reinforce the same old stereotypes and divisions?

The '70s were a fascinating time to listen to the possibilities. During this decade, musicians such as Marvin Gaye, Curtis Mayfield, and George Clinton consciously chose to use their music as an instrument of change. But each did so with a different approach and in a different context.

Gaye came out of the environment of Motown where overt political messages had always been a no-no. He fought against that system and won. Mayfield had been a main exponent of unity music but his brand of uplifting pop took a radical U-turn in the '70s. And Clinton, through his bands Parliament and Funkadelic, sought to eradicate the notions of categorizable music altogether.

The tantalizing possibility of people transcending prejudice through song was one of the headiest dreams of the 1970s, and for a few shining moments, it looked as if that dream were possible. The decade saw upbeat pop hits like the O'Jays' "Love Train" and Johnny Nash's "I Can See Clearly Now" take the message of racial solidarity into the realm of joyous celebration and reverie.

The "Love Train" the O'Jays sang about made stops everywhere. It went beyond the historical racial divide in America and circumnavigated the globe. "Tell all the folks in Egypt and Israel, too," the group sang with gentle urgency, "please don't miss this train at the station."

*The O'Jays*

In one perfect three-minute single written by the great Philly Soul team of Kenny Gamble and Leon Huff, "Love Train" summed up the goals of unity music without resorting to the pie-in-the-sky idealism of John Lennon's "Imagine" or the simplistic notions of Three Dog Night's "Black & White."

"Love Train" achieved a notable distinction for a soul record when it was released in 1975—it reached number one on both the R&B and pop charts. This meant, in the parlance of the music industry, the song had crossed over. The term "crossing over," in blunt terms, meant white people were buying recordings made by black performers.

Even in the '70s, a group of African-American musicians could not afford to take this kind of success for granted. Having a crossover hit meant the O'Jays would be invited to appear on TV variety shows like *The Sonny and Cher Show* and *The Flip Wilson Show* and that Top 40 radio stations would be playing their records.

A song that managed to cross those barriers, in a small way, loosened another brick in the wall of prejudice—prejudice was evident in the way music stores divided their music bins into seperate racial categories. And that is why crossing over became such a crucial achievement.

Without the crossover dream, there could be no integration. Perhaps Berry Gordy understood the implications of this equation better than anyone else. Gordy's

Motown label was the crossroads for the crossover. Since the early '60s, Gordy had lorded over a stable of talent unparalleled in modern pop music including the Four Tops, the Temptations, Martha and the Vandellas, the Supremes, Stevie Wonder, Marvin Gaye, Smokey Robinson and the Miracles, and the Jackson Five.

## Number One Hits on Both R&B and Pop Charts

*Berry Gordy*

**1970**
I Want You Back—Jackson 5
Ain't No Mountain High Enough—Diana Ross
The Tears of a Clown—Smokey Robinson & The Miracles

**1971**
Just My Imagination (Running Away With Me)—Temptations
Want Ads—Honey Cone
Family Affair—Sly & The Family Stone

**1972**
Let's Stay Together—Al Green
Lean On Me—Bill Withers
Me and Mrs. Jones—Billy Paul

**1973**
Superstition—Stevie Wonder
Love Train—O'Jays
Midnight Train to Georgia—Gladys Knight & The Pips

**1974**
Feeling Like Makin' Love—Roberta Flack
Can't Get Enough Of Your Love, Babe—Barry White
You Haven't Done Nothin—Stevie Wonder

**1975**
Lady Marmalade—Labelle
The Hustle—Van McCoy & The Soul City Symphony
Fly, Robin, Fly—Silver Convention

**1976**
Boogie Fever—Sylvers
Love Hangover—Diana Ross
Play That Funky Music—Wild Cherry

**1977**
I Wish—Stevie Wonder
Car Wash—Rose Royce
Don't Leave Me This Way—Thelma Houston

**1978**
Three Times A Lady—Commodores
Boogie Oogie Oogie—Taste Of Honey
Le Freak—Chic

**1979**
Reunited—Peaches & Herb
Bad Girls—Donna Summer
Good Times—Chic

Through hit songs like "Dancing in the Streets," Motown had always endorsed a message of passive resistance when it came to fighting prejudice. The music itself was the message. There was no overt attempt to preach about unity and togetherness. In fact, under Gordy's watchful eye anything that might grate against this sensibility was deliberately expurgated.

*Marvin Gaye desired a new image*

For years, no political issues or current events were allowed to interfere with the creation of party music at Motown. But by the early 1970s, after the social climate of the country had undergone radical changes (Detroit, the home of Motown, was the site of some of the worst race riots in U.S. history in the late '60s) Gordy's famous short-leash policy began to loosen.

One of the first products of Motown's new enlightenment was Marvin Gaye's landmark 1971 album *What's Going On*. The healing tone of this soulful masterpiece—soft, angelic choirs, billowing conga beats—sent a strong universalist message through both its music and its lyrics, inveighing against war, environmental waste, and a society where violence and animosity had become accepted facts of everyday life.

*What's Going On* was a wholly authentic and impassioned cry for tolerance. Gaye took the opportunity to address the audience he knew best—the black audience. "Brother, brother, brother" he lamented, "there's far too many of you dying." The messages of *What's Going On* were aimed at the problems of the inner-city— economic hardship, black-on-black violence, and the racial divide.

As Motown's guiding light and CEO, Gordy was understandably worried about the effect of *What's Going On.* Orienting Motown in a more political direction was a calculated risk. By releasing an album that addressed so many hot-button issues, Gordy might have forfeited the crossover dream he and so many others had worked so long to erect. At least that was his fear.

Happily for Gordy, *What's Going On* was greeted by critical acclaim, three top ten singles, and a number-one album. After its success, Gordy cautiously began to loosen the creative reigns on his other artists. For example, Norman Whitfield was allowed to produce more politically slanted material for the Temptations, including the classics "Ball of Confusion" and "Papa Was a Rollin' Stone."

By and large, however, Motown still produced a vision of unity. In 1971, Stevie Wonder sang a cover version of the Beatles' classic "We Can Work it Out," and this was the philosophy that Gordy would stick to. Even after he opened the floodgates and allowed Wonder to record edgier songs such as "Higher Ground," "You Haven't Done Nothin'," and "Living in the City," only a few Motown artists were allowed to push the envelope like James Brown or George Clinton.

There was a certain irony about the predicament that Gordy and Motown found themselves in. More and more, the burden of making music that bridged the racial divide and promoted a message of tolerance was left to black artists and black-

*Big Stevie Wonder*

owned labels such as Motown, Gamble and Huff's Philadelphia International, and Curtis Mayfield's Curtom Records. There was an inequality about pushing equality, a contradiction that did not go unnoticed among musicians. "I just want to ask a question," sang Marvin Gaye on "Save the Children," "Who really cares to save the world in despair?"

Another compelling question facing artists who sang about unity was who exactly was their audience? It was a fine line, after all, between catering to the so-called

"crossover dream" and ignoring the problems in your own backyard. You could sing all you wanted to about saving the world, but if you alienated the mainstream audience, you were out of business.

That's why Gordy's decision to move his operations from Detroit to Los Angeles in 1972 was symbolic: it exposed the truth about the bifurcation of black society in America. On one hand, Gordy wanted to produce movies, and to do so he had to move away from his roots and infiltrate the center of power of white America. On the other hand, by assimilating into that world, he was relinquishing a part of Motown's identity.

The move from Detroit to Los Angeles spoke volumes about a hidden reality in the music business. Two separate and unequal markets existed for black artists: (1) the crossover market targeted to black and white audiences, and (2) the black community alone. Although both options were economically viable, the latter meant relinquishing the dream that music could appeal to all people.

Perhaps Gordy was reluctant to acknowledge the limits of the crossover dream or to market specifically to African-Americans. But artists like James Brown apparently felt no such reticence. As the self-described "Godfather of Soul," Brown had always spoken directly to his audience. And in 1969, he was undoubtedly summing up the feelings of many of his most loyal fans when he sang "I Don't Want Nobody To Give Me Nothing (Open Up the Door, I'll Get It Myself)."

Preaching self-reliance, Brown provided a nonstop soundtrack of black issues. As the '70s progressed, he provided a breathtaking grab bag of stylistic innovations. Prefiguring rap music by a full decade, Brown dropped the classical song structure of melody and relied on rhythm and words to drive his point across, thus breaking

the holy rule of Western musical conventions (melody) and returning to the roots of African expression (rhythm).

Brown had long since proven that identity music—if that's the term that adequately describes songs like "Say It Loud—I'm Black and I'm Proud" and "Soul Power"—was economically viable. "The Payback," as Brown put it, wasn't just a call for retribution, it was also a demand for reparations.

Gil Scott-Heron, who released the classic song "The Revolution Will Not Be Televised" in 1970, was another voice of defiance. He captured the frustration that many African-Americans were feeling about getting a piece of the economic pie. In "Whitey on the Moon" Scott-Heron addressed these concerns in a fiery proto-rap that concluded:

> With all that money I made last year
> For whitey on the moon
> How come I ain't got no money here?
> Whitey's on the moon
> You know I just about had my fill
> Of whitey on the moon
> I think I'll send these doctor's bills
> Airmail special to whitey on the moon

The moral outrage of Gil Scott-Heron and groups like The Last Poets was a potent form of expressing the rage and anger many felt. This represented a point of view that could not be ignored. The diminishing returns of the Great Society and the rift between the races, to some people, seemed forever unbridgeable and for this and other reasons, artists like Scott-Heron had no desire to crossover.

But where was the bridge—a voice of conscience who could find some commonality among the different races and yet give full expression to the black experience? The answer, oddly enough, came in the form of a soundtrack called *Superfly* that followed the exploits of a Harlem drug dealer.

This was no ordinary soundtrack. Written and performed by Curtis Mayfield, it was a masterpiece of moral persuasion. On songs like the title track, "Pusherman," and

"Freddy's Dead," Mayfield maintained an almost journalistic objectivity about the events unfolding on the screen, neither glorifying the violence and the drug-dealing nor preaching in a high-handed way about the consequences.

Music provided the message. And the music of the *Superfly* soundtrack was irresistible, featuring powerful horn charts, propulsive polyrhythms and Mayfield's trademark *wah-wah* guitar effects. The soundtrack, which earned the composer an Academy Award, remains a cornerstone of '70s music and a unique product of its time.

The lyrics of Mayfield's music in *Superfly* sent a dramatically different message than the plot of the film, which was a stereotypical example of a then-popular genre of black action films—a.k.a. "blaxploitation"—which offered gritty, authentic slices of ghetto life with plentiful amounts of violence and sex. It would have been inconceivable for Mayfield to glorify the exploits of pimps, pushers, and gangsters, however.

This kind of decision was nothing new for Mayfield. As a member of The Impressions, he had long established himself as a voice of conscience within—and outside—the black community, and perhaps more than any other musician of his era, he could be considered the standard-bearer of the ideal of unity through song.

Instead of singing from a pulpit, Mayfield always spoke directly to "brothers and sisters" on Impression classics such as "Keep on Pushing" and "We're a Winner." One of Mayfield's greatest pleas for tolerance was "People Get Ready," a precursor to "Love Train" (and, for that matter, Cat Stevens' "Peace Train"), which used the metaphor of a passenger locomotive to symbolize the propulsive force of people coming together. "Don't need no baggage," Mayfield sang, "you just get on board."

For the most part, Mayfield's songs had been inspirational hymns, free of invective and incendiary emotion. But, in 1970, he announced a new direction with a single

*Curtis Mayfield*

called, "If There's A Hell Below We're All Going to Go," which began with the chilling shout: "Sisters! Niggers! Whiteys! Jews! Crackers!"

The lyrics of "If There's A Hell Below" were less optimistic than his previous songs, hinting rather obviously that patience had its limits. Musically, the song also had an ominous tone. With its fuzz-bass, conga drum beats, and Mayfield's scratchy guitar, the song was a precursor to the apocalyptic sound of his future work on *Superfly*.

"If There's A Hell Below We're All Going to Go" was a pivotal moment in the unity-music movement. It gave a voice to the resignation of those who were struggling for equality and inclusion, and at the same time, it had that purifying Mayfield touch. By warning of the anger that was brewing, Mayfield emphasized that everybody would

*Sly Stone*

suffer the consequences of not addressing the problems afflicting the underclass. Like the title said, hell didn't discriminate.

Many artists joined Mayfield in expressing their anger and frustration, including Sly Stone, whose resolutely sunny plea for tolerance of "Everyday People" had been a number one hit for the Family Stone in 1969. From the sound of things, Stone was feeling less optimistic about unity.

His classic 1971 album, *There's a Riot Goin' On*, reflected this change. Where "Everyday People" was a bright vision of a colorblind society, the music of *There's a Riot Goin' On* was a defiant message aimed at exposing the limits of such an idealistic approach. From now on, Stone sang, it was a "Family Affair"— a song from the album that, ironically enough, crossed-over and reached number one on the pop charts.

"Family Affair" had an air of heavy resignation. And that sense of weariness was a particularly acute commentary coming from a musician whose energized performance of "I Want to Take You Higher" was a highlight of the Woodstock Festival. But on *There's a Riot Goin' On*, Stone was clearly aiming his music to black audiences (sample title: "Africa Talks To You") and explicitly rejecting the more-utopian notions of his previous work.

But unlike Mayfield, who always made a point to sing to "brothers and sisters," Stone seemed overwhelmed by the pressures of balancing his image as a good-time performer with the weightier concerns of the struggle for equal rights. When he grew increasingly eccentric and declined into substance abuse, his tailspin was both a personal tragedy and a great loss for music.

Mayfield, on the other hand, had labored too long and too hard to allow anger and disillusionment to overwhelm his greater goals. "Too many have died in protecting my pride for me to go second class," he sang on "This Is My Country," a 1970 single from Mayfield's own Curtom label.

Like Gordy before him, Mayfield had taken economic control over his career by starting Curtom. Self-reliance was a key component of the crossover dream and, therefore, an essential element in the cause of unity. Without a promise of equal footing and economic improvement in people's lives, one of the only avenues left would be the gangster lifestyle of *Superfly*. But Mayfield nailed the message stone cold: gangster life had consequences, and while exciting, it wasn't something to be celebrated and imitated. Through his own perseverance and dedication, Mayfield demonstrated there was a better way.

If Curtis Mayfield was the voice of reason in the cause of unity music then George Clinton was the voice of un-reason. In the two bands he concurrently fronted, Parliament and Funkadelic, Clinton deliberately reveled in the theater of the absurd. Album titles such as *Maggot Brain, Cosmic Slop,* and *Free Your Mind and Your Ass Will Follow* said all you needed to know.

Absurdity was Clinton's path to the great enlightenment, and perhaps his greatest contribution to music was his willingness to laugh at himself. While some people found his nursery-rhyme lyrics childish, they were, in a way, his most brilliant stylistic innovation. By reducing the lyrical content to nonsense, Clinton sidestepped the obvious pitfalls of unity music and preached a gospel whose message was stripped down to its essence: let's party.

Everyone could join in—that was the message of Funkadelic's classic album *One Nation Under a Groove*. But in no way was the message a concession. Quite the opposite. Funkadelic was proudly African-American—in-your-face, rhythm-based and stoned. It was a radical mix, and with his multi-colored dreadlocks swinging to and fro, Clinton was the leader of the three-ring circus.

In the annals of music, it is difficult to imagine a more unlikely hero for bringing together the races. But Clinton had a vision. "Fear is at the root of man's destruction of himself," he wrote in the liner notes to *Maggot Brain* and this bit of wisdom

"You know how they say that the teenyboppers and the old heads don't get along?" asks George (Clinton). "We've actually bridged that gap. The older ones sit up in the bleachers and smoke their joints and be a little cooler, and the geepies get out on the floor, checkin' us out, but it isn't like the kind of separation you'd see between a Grateful Dead audience and a Kiss audience. It's just one of the miracles Funk can perform. . . ."
—*George Clinton Interview,* Creem, *Vol. 8, #11, April 1977*

*Do we know that strife of every kind increases as hatred, resentment, jealousy and prejudice increase, and that all these stem from one thing only: Fear? And do we know that one thing only ensures the escalation of the spiral of violence and destruction; our own unwillingness to recognize the full extent of our fear and its effects— our fear of Fear?*

*For each and every one of us, as long as he is afraid, and unwilling to see with full clarity his fear for what it is, contributes to the crippling conflict that has become the hallmark of this world of ours.*

—*Liner Notes from Maggot Brain*

spoke volumes about his approach. Clinton *was* fearless. He not only asked "Who Says a Funk Band Can't Play Rock!" but set out to prove it wasn't true. Backed by Eddie Hazel's guitar pyrotechnics and showcasing a revolutionary mix of funk, soul, and gospel influences, Funkadelic dropped the bomb.

But beneath the wild theatrics and the sheer bravado, Clinton and his cohorts, by making inclusionary music, were insisting to be included. "Chocolate City"—a classic Parliament track—drove this point home to hilarious effect. "They still call it the White House but that's a temporary condition," Clinton rapped, imagining Muhammad Ali as the president, Richard Pryor as the minister of education, Stevie Wonder as the secretary of fine arts, and Aretha Franklin as the first lady.

"Chocolate City" was a reality check. Middle class African-Americans were making strides ("gaining on ya," the group sang in unison on the song's chorus) and although not everyone was sharing in this newfound prosperity, this fact needed to be addressed and acknowledged. "A chocolate city is no dream," Clinton informed his audience, "it's my piece of the rock."

Although Parliament and Funkadelic never shied away from speaking their minds, the cause of unity was never far from the heart of Clinton's quirky vision. Could we all get down, as he promised, for the funk of it?

The key word in the equation was funk. Its propulsive groove, featuring hard rock guitar and bubbling bass lines, promised a radical crossroads, if not a crossover. And apparently, as witnessed by the sudden proliferation of white bands playing funk, a lot of people other than African-Americans were up for the downstroke: Wild Cherry ("Play That Funky Music"), Average White Band ("Pick up the Pieces"), David Bowie ("Fame"), and KC and the Sunshine Band ("Get Down Tonight").

On the other side of the equation, funk acts like Earth, Wind & Fire ("Shining Star"), the Ohio Players ("Fire"), and Rose Royce ("Car Wash") all scored number-one hits on *Billboard*'s pop charts in the '70s. Something was crossing over, and its name was funk. Why funk? Perhaps its popularity was due to an insistence on maintaining its standing as good-time party music. The "we" of "we're gonna have a funky good time" was inclusionary. It took James Brown's message of identity one step further, tossed aside concerns of difference and race, and exhorted everybody to chant: "Say it loud, I'm funky and proud."

An evolved sense of self-worth was a key to the crossover dream. When Earth, Wind & Fire sang "you're a shining star, no matter who you are," it reminded people that celebrating their diversity as well as their commonality remained the ultimate promise of unity music. And, although the inevitable split in the markets continued, signs of evolution and change were everywhere. White kids were watching *Soul Train* as intently as black kids had watched *American Bandstand*.

In a sense, these changes could be seen as validating Berry Gordy's original dream of creating one market devoid of color or race. The Jackson 5, one of his last great dis-

coveries, were the perfect example of the formula. Their brand of immaculate "bubble-gum soul" crossed all boundaries.

The Jackson 5's first four singles—"ABC," "I Want You Back," "The Love You Save," and "I'll Be There"—were arguably as well-crafted and tuneful as the corresponding output by the Beatles. And wunderkind Michael Jackson became a new kind of colorblind hero. Whether starring in the movie version of *The Wiz*, an all-black version of *The Wizard of Oz* that opened in 1975, or perfecting the smooth disco moves of his late-1970s album *Off the Wall*, Jackson was a superstar without labels (at least in the '70s).

Poised between the great promise of the civil rights victories and the freedom which came with economic self-dependence, it was, as the group Chic sang, "Good Times." At least briefly—before the backlash set in; a backlash, ironically, in which "Good Times" would figure prominently.

"Good Times" was a classic crossover hit—a number one on both the pop and R&B charts in 1979. Chic's inclusive, celebratory ode to join in the fun proved that some-

*Chic*

thing had crossed over. But what was that something? "Good Times" was a disco hit—not soul, not funk—but disco. And disco, it turns out, would have a shattering effect on the crossover dream.

"Disco sucks" was the chant that changed everything. Despite its promise to breach the racial divide, disco resulted in a backlash. Radio stations began shying away from black records to avoid the disco label (the FM radio format known as Album-Oriented Rock almost never played black music, except for songs by Jimi Hendrix), and by 1980, the percentage of songs which charted on both the pop and R&B charts fell to an all-time low.

Ironically, it turns out that white teenage boys living in the suburbs and black, teenage boys living in the city had something in common: they both felt alienated by disco. The former felt threatened for a variety of reasons (see "Bad Girls, Good Times, Freak Out!"). The latter resented disco for flaunting a lavish lifestyle they couldn't afford.

But showing great invention, a few teenagers in the South Bronx rectified that problem by rhyming lyrics over twelve-inch disco records playing on turntables. One of the most popular of those records was "Good Times," which as it turns out, became the underpinning of the first rap hit, "Rapper's Delight" by the Sugar Hill Gang.

Released in October 1979, "Rapper's Delight" subsequently became the biggest selling twelve-inch single of all time and the cornerstone of the hip-hop industry. But while rap could (and would) be seen as reinforcing all of the lessons of the cross over dream—for example, Sugar Hill Records, which released "Rapper's Delight," was a black-owned and operated label—its legacy as unity music would turn out to be a good deal more ambiguous.

As the last significant musical movement of the '70s, rap is highly symbolic about what was achieved and what wasn't achieved in the cause of unity music. What was achieved was an unprecedented convergence of audiences. Funk, soul, R&B, disco, and finally rap all achieved a degree of crossover success that would have seemed impossible at the beginning of the decade.

What failed was the endurance of the message. The rise of gangster rap proved that the crossover dream, for most African-Americans, was still a mirage and that a color blind society was easier to evoke in a three-minute pop single than in reality. This was never more clear than in 1992, when a nervous-looking Rodney King came to the microphone in an effort to calm down the riots in Los Angeles that had resulted after an all-white jury had acquitted four cops of beating him and haltingly asked "Can't we all just get along?"

That message sounded strangely familiar. Almost fifteen years earlier, a racially integrated band out of Compton, California, had asked a strikingly similar question: "Why Can't We Be Friends?" Apparently, all those years later, the question had yet to be answered. But the battle for unity was still underway, and perhaps in retrospect, the band's name War had really made sense all along.

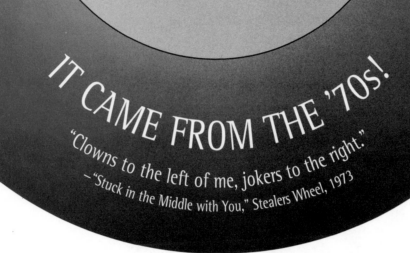

# IT CAME FROM THE '70s!

*"Clowns to the left of me, jokers to the right."*
—"Stuck in the Middle with You," Stealers Wheel, 1973

A bunch of strange rumors spread in the '70s. It was said that Mikey from the Life cereal commercial drank some Coke, ate some Pop Rocks, and exploded. A back-up singer for the Ohio Players, it was widely rumored, had been electrocuted during the recording of "Love Rollercoaster." And then there was the nasty scuttlebutt about Rod Stewart, and the various reasons he had to have his stomach pumped.

None of these rumors were ever substantiated, of course. But *everything* seemed believable in the '70s. A newspaper heiress could be kidnapped by Symbionese Liberation Army and then turn around and begin robbing banks in broad daylight. Where was Symbiona and why did they need liberating? Why even ask? There was no answer. It was just that kind of decade. You had to accept that fact and get on with your life.

*Leo Sayer's haircut. It just was.*

There were some aspects of the '70s that just defied rational explanation. Like Leo Sayer's haircut—it just was. You could analyze it for days, months, years, but what was the point? In the end you were bound to throw your hands in the air and sigh, "only in the '70s." And those four little words said it all. They expressed the inexpressible, described the indescribable, and explained the unexplainable—which was fortunate because there was a lot of explaining to do.

Fondue sets. CB radios. Bean bags. Soap-on-a-rope. The AMC Pacer. Linda Blair. "The Gong Show." Billy Beer. Fern bars. Iron-on decals. Pet rocks. Platform shoes. The Ronco slicer-dicer. Leisure suits. K-tel Presents. Don Kirshner. The Nixon double-victory sign. The pompatus of love. And on and on and on.

## The Top 10 Singles of 1974

1. "The Way We Were" - Barbra Streisand
2. "Come and Get Your Love" - Redbone
3. "Seasons In The Sun" - Terry Jacks
4. "Show And Tell" - Al Wilson
5. "Love's Theme" - The Love Unlimited Orchestra
6. "Locomotion" - Grand Funk Railroad
7. "Bennie and the Jets" - Elton John
8. "You Make Me Feel Brand New" - The Stylistics
9. "Sunshine On My Shoulder" - John Denver
10. "T.S.O.P." - MFSB

People have characterized the '70s as irrational, out of kilter, bizarre. And just one listen to the lyrics of "Seasons in the Sun" (#1 on the *Billboard* charts in 1974) by Terry Jacks will tell you more than a cultural historian could in a long, scholarly treatise:

> *Good-bye to you, my trusted friend*
> *We've known each other since we were nine or ten*
> *Together we've climbed hills and trees*
> *Learned of love and ABCs*
> *Skinned our hearts and skinned our knees*

Sung with plaintive resignation, Jack's 1974 hit told the tale of a young man dying of a terminal illness. But there was something quirky about the lyrics by pop poet Rod McKuen. Some were depressing ("good-bye, pa-pa, it's hard to die") but some were positive and upbeat ("we had joy, we had fun, we had seasons in the sun") so it ended up sounding like the cheeriest song about death ever written.

But that was the nature of the decade. Throughout the '70s, all sorts of out-of-whack melodramatic oddities hit the pop charts. On "Run Joey Run" (#4, 1975) by David Geddes a father is gunning for his daughter's boyfriend but shoots her by mistake. On "Billy, Don't Be a Hero" (#1, 1974) by Bo Donaldson and the Heywoods the boyfriend ignores his girlfriend's advice, goes off to war, and gets shot.

Random bits of whimsy? Unconnected to reality? You could be forgiven for making that assumption; but most of these strange little nuggets are actually the essence of that peculiar thing we call "only in the '70s." That is the unique thing about all of the fads and phenomena of the 1970s. Each passing trend—disco, CB radio, streaking, Kung Fu movies, *Star Wars*, hot-pants, King Tut, junk food—had a moment in the sun on the *Billboard* charts.

*Danny Bonaduce. One with the '70s.*

For example, when the Tutankhamen exhibit toured America, Steve Martin scored the novelty hit, "King Tut" (#17, 1978); when fast-food franchises began proliferating in every mini-mall across the country, Larry Groce wrote "Junk Food Junkie" (#9, 1976); and when John Travolta clones began invading the local discos and imitating his finger-thrusting dance moves, Rick Dees released "Disco Duck" (#1, 1976).

In a way there is something oddly charming about a decade that memorialized its peculiarities in song. But that doesn't mean that pop music just ignored all the other issues affecting society. In fact, it was quite the opposite. Much of the social history of the decade was captured indelibly in popular music, but always with that special "only in the '70s" twist.

This was the decade, after all, where Barry Manilow sang "I Write The Songs" (#1, 1976) even though "the song" was written by Bruce Johnston. Some things defy explanation, and so it is with the '70s. Fortunately for us, the singers and songwriters made sure we would remember every crazy quirk.

# *Streaking* · · · · · · · · · · · · · · · · · ·

Streaking is a perfect example of how music memorialized a trend which otherwise would have been fleeting. Before Robert Opel decided to bare all and streak across the stage live at the Academy Awards on April 4, 1974, streaking was seen as one of those passing fads, like telephone-booth stuffing, which periodically swept through college campuses, and disappeared. After Opel's global exposure, a full-fledged phenomenon was underway.

Sure enough, only eleven days after the Oscar telecast, Ray Stevens released "The Streak" (#1, 1974), a happy-go-lucky tale of a mad streaker and his acts of exhibitionism. The narrator of the song captured the mixed emotions many people felt about streaking, an attitude of bemusement along with a touch of the puritanical ("Don't look Ethel!").

# Native American Awareness • • • • • • •

Thanks to the Academy Awards another '70s trend made headlines: protesting the mistreatment of Native Americans. Marlon Brando's refusal to accept his Best Actor award for *The Godfather* on the grounds that the film industry continued to exploit the image of Native Americans helped bring this cause to the fore.

Brando's Oscar snub was just one incident in a decade-long history of political agitation for Native American rights in the '70s, including the occupations at Wounded Knee and Alcatraz Island. As always, pop music, in its slightly offbeat way, conveyed

*Sacheen Littlefeather holding Marlon Brando's rejection letter. It was later revealed she was not a Native American, but Maria Cruz, the former "Miss American Vampire of 1970."*

some of the relevant sentiments of this period, including the Raiders' version of John D. Loudermilk's "Indian Reservation (The Lament of the Cherokee Reservation Indian)" (#1, 1971).

On a superficial level, the Raider's hit song reflected the public's growing awareness about the mistreatment of Native Americans. But, oddly, the defiant lyrics ("Cherokee people, Cherokee tribe, so proud to live, so proud to die") were being sung by guys who wore tri-cornered Colonial hats and American Revolutionary garb earlier in their careers.

# Interracial Love ....................

"Indian Reservation" demonstrated how serious matters could be reduced to cartoons on the pop charts. Another example was the love between people of different races. First there was Three Dog Night's paean to togetherness "Black & White" (#1, 1972) whose chorus went: "the child is black, the child is white." And then there was the Stories, whose tale of an illicit love affair on "Brother Louie" (#1, 1973) began with a strangely familiar observation: "She was black as the night, Louie was whiter than white." White, black, black, white. Deep, huh?

# Multiracial Children ...............

Even stranger was the "half-breed" phenomenon, an off-shoot of Native American awareness movement. The point of departure for this trend was a series of vigilante films based on the character Billy Jack, the karate-chopping multiracial hero played by actor Tom Laughlin. The first in the series of these sleeper hits featured Coven's "One Tin Soldier" (#26, 1971), a song whose irony mirrored the film's mixed message of peace through retribution with lyrics such as: "Go ahead and hate your neighbor, go ahead and cheat a friend."

But "One Tin Soldier" sounded positively enlightened compared to Cher's "Half-Breed" (#1, 1973). Having already mined the oppressed-and-downtrodden territory with 1971's "Gypsys, Tramps & Thieves," Cher gave an emotional reading to the tale of the outcast daughter of a Cherokee mother and a white father. Her follow-up hit, "Dark Lady"—despite the title—was not about a victimized half-person-of-color but instead told the story of a philandering soothsayer. Go figure.

# *Divorce, American Style* • • • • • • • • • •

Cher was always a harbinger of things to come. In the mid-70s, she announced she was splitting up with Sonny Bono, thus ending their celebrated marriage and TV variety show. The tabloids were abuzz with the inside scoop. Three days after her divorce papers came through, Cher married Gregg Allman of the Allman Brothers to great sensation—and then divorced him ten days later to even greater sensation.

*Gregg Allman: I've got you, babe. Cher: That's what you think.*

Was it really shocking? It shouldn't have been—divorce rates were skyrocketing. As usual, the pop charts reflected the trends of the culture at large. Paul Simon's "50 Ways to Leave Your Lover" (#1, 1976) managed to put a light-hearted spin on breaking up. But, for sheer pathos, "Daddy Don't You Walk So Fast" (#4, 1972) blew away the competition. The tear-jerking smash for Wayne Newton concerned a father confronting his daughter as he is about to leave town and break up his marriage. Sung with Vegas-like verve by Newton, it was a triple-hankie special:

> The love between the two of us was dying
> And it got so bad I knew I had to leave
> But halfway down that highway, when I turned around I saw
> My little daughter running after me crying
> Daddy, don't you walk so fast.

Of course, being the great guy that he is, Wayne can't bring himself to leave ("I couldn't bear to hear those words again"), so he turns around and attempts to reconcile "with the mother of my child" for the sake of his daughter. Yes, even in Wayne's world, love means never having to say you're sorry.

# Rock Marriages • • • • • • • • • • • • • • • •

Oddly enough, marriage became something of a career move during the '70s. First, there was the husband-and-wife team of Daryl Dragon and Toni Tennille—a.k.a., Captain & Tennille—who sang "Love Will Keep Us Together" (#1, 1975). There was also the celebrated singer/songwriter union of Carly Simon and James Taylor, who sang "Devoted to You" (#36, 1978).

Despite cooing pledges of fidelity and claims of everlasting love, Simon and Taylor ended up in divorce court. But their unsuccessful union was nothing compared to the double-disaster marriages of ABBA and Fleetwood Mac.

The former was formed when ("A") Agnetha Falkstog married ("B") Bjorn Ulvaeus and ("B") Benny Andersson married ("A") Anni-Frid Lyngstad. A double-marriage Swedish super-group; how '70s! But ABBA's frosty pop gave little indication of the strain the couples were experiencing. They just kept smiling.

Fleetwood Mac's ill-fated husband-and-wife teams, Lindsey Buckingham and Stevie Nicks and John and Christine McVie, were not nearly as reticent. On *Rumours*, their best-selling 1977 album, the group used every chance it had to sing about their state of emotional duress, most vividly on Buckingham's blistering kiss-off to Nicks (who provided back-up vocals) on "Go Your Own Way" (#10, 1977).

Since this is already the best-selling group in the universe, I finally have an answer when people ask me to name The Next Big Thing. What I wonder is how we can head them off at the airport. Plan A: Offer Bjorn and Benny the leads in Beatlemania ( how could they resist the honor?). Plan B: Appoint Bjorn the head of the U. N. and Benny his pilot (or vice-versa) and replace them with John Lennon and Paul McCartney. Plan C: Overexpose them in singing commercials.

—*Robert Christgau, review of ABBA's*
*Arrival album,* Village Voice, *1977*

*ABBA dabba do!*

## Feminist Rock · · · · · · · · · · · · · · · · · · ·

The marital discord that formed *Rumours* must have hit a nerve, as evidenced by worldwide sales of more than 25 million copies. But after all, the '70s was the decade of the "Battle of the Sexes," the 1973 grudge match between male chauvinist Bobby Riggs and female tennis star Billy Jean King, who soundly thrashed Riggs in a live, national broadcast at the Houston Astrodome.

The drive for women's rights was one of the defining political movements of the 1970s. Pop music managed to honor the feminist movement and dishonor it, sometimes in the same song. There was, of course, "I Am Woman" (#1, 1972), Helen Reddy's famous ode to female solidarity that inadvertently provided one of those "only in the '70s" moments when Reddy got up to accept her Grammy Award and thanked God "because *She* makes everything possible."

The television equivalent of Reddy's magnum opus was the appearance of super-heroines like Lindsay Wagner ("The Bionic Woman") and Lynda Carter ("Wonder Woman"). The latter used "feminum" to unleash her unearthly superpowers. She also had an unforgettable theme song:

> *Wonder Woman, Wonder Woman*
> *In your satin tights*
> *Fighting for your rights*
> *And the old red, white, and blue . . .*

# *TV Theme Songs* • • • • • • • • • • • • • •

Only in the '70s could TV and music merge to confront the social issues of the time and make a complete mockery of it in the process. But that was the embodiment of that uniquely American art form—the TV theme song.

The '70s were a golden era for TV themes. Their peak year on the *Billboard* charts was 1976, when Cyndi Grecco's "Making Our Dreams Come True" (from "Laverne & Shirley") peaked at #25, Pratt & McLain's "Happy Days" charted at #5, and John Sebastian's "Welcome Back, Kotter" went all the way to #1.

Certain TV themes tried to inject a social message into the proceedings. For example, "Maude" ("right on, Maude") and "The Mary Tyler Moore Show" ("you're going to

*The Jeffersons: Movin' on up!*

make it after all") were full of feminist subtext, while "Good Times" ("temporary lay-offs/easy credit rip-offs") and "The Jeffersons" ("We're moving on up/To the great deluxe apartment in the sky") reflected the decay and renewal of urban life.

And some TV themes were even poignant. For example, Jose Feliciano's "Chico and the Man," a gentle ballad about a Mexican-American mechanic coming to terms with his boss ("Chico don't be discouraged/The man he ain't so hard to understand") became almost unbearably sad when Freddie Prinze, the popular star of the show, took his own life in 1977.

# Crime Show Themes

As rates of crime began soaring in the '70s, TV Westerns with law and order motifs, such as "Bonanza" and "Gunsmoke," fell out of favor. They were replaced by the slick, urban one-named detective: Kojak, Columbo, Ironside, Baretta, McCloud, Harry-O, Mannix, McMillan, Banacek, and Quincy.

Several crime show themes made the pop charts, including Mike Post's "Theme From 'The Rockford Files'" (#10, 1975) and Rhythm Heritage's "Theme From 'S.W.A.T.'" (#1, 1976). And who can forget that "only in the '70s" moment when David Soul, of "Starsky and Hutch" fame, scored a number-one smash in 1977 with the fabulously mawkish and feathery ballad "Don't Give Up on Us Baby."

# Movie Themes

Music that came out of the movies, while generally less socially relevant than TV themes, also provided a distinctly '70s flavor to the decade: the down-home bluegrass of "Dueling Banjos" (#2, 1973) from *Deliverance*; the ominous "bum bum bum bum" of "Theme From *Jaws*" (#32, 1975); and the crackling Academy Award winning funk workouts, Curtis Mayfield's *Superfly* (#8, 1972) and Isaac Hayes' "Theme from *Shaft*" (#1, 1971).

The latter record had perhaps the most unforgettable musical Q&A of the decade: "Who's the black private dick that's a sex machine to all the chicks? Shaft! Can you dig it? Right on."

Isaac Hayes

*Shaft* and *Superfly* were representative of a genre of movies called "blaxploitation," or black action films. Other film themes came to represent popular genres of the

## Blaxploitation Movies In the '70s:

**1970**
Cotton Comes to Harlem

**1971**
Shaft
Sweet Sweetback's Baad Assss Song

**1972**
Blacula
Black Gunn
Black Mama, White Mama
Come Back, Charleston Blue
Cool Breeze
Hammer
Shaft's Big Score!
Superfly

**1973**
Blackenstein
Black Caesar
Black Godfather
Cleopatra Jones
Coffy

Hell Up in Harlem
The Mack
Scream, Blacula, Scream
Shaft in Africa
Slaughter's Big Rip-Off
Superfly T.N.T.
Sweet Jesus, Preacherman

**1974**
Black Belt Jones
Black Eye
Foxy Brown
Super Dude
Three Tough Guys
T.N.T. Jackson
Trucker Turner
Willie Dynamite

**1975**
Adios Amigo
Black Bikers from Hell
Black Jesus

Black Lolita
Black Samson
Bucktown
Cleopatra Jones and the Casino of Gold
Dolemite
Mandingo
Sheba Baby

**1976**
Black Fist
Black Shampoo
Cooley High
Dr. Black and Mr. Hyde
Mean Johnny Barrows

**1977**
Black Samuri

**1978**
Black Eliminator

**1979**
Disco Godfather

decade. Meco's "*Star Wars* Theme" (#1, 1977) represented space epics; Bill Conti's "Gonna Fly Now" (#1, 1977) from *Rocky* represented the underdog comeback film; Andy Williams' "Theme From *Love Story*" (#9, 1971) represented terminal-illness movies; Maureen McGovern's "Morning After" (#1, 1973) represented disaster films; and who can forget Mike Oldfield's chilling "Tubular Bells" (#7, 1974), which represented the pea-soup-and-oatmeal vomit devil-worship classic *The Exorcist*?

Another genre of movies was "the animals are attacking," which included scream-fests such as *Night of the Lepus* (rabbits), *Squirm* (worms), *Stanley* (snakes), *Frogs* (frogs), and *C.H.O.M.P.S.* (robot dogs). The most popular films of this genre were *Willard* (rats) and its sequel *Ben* (more rats). The latter movie featured Michael Jackson's tender ode to the rodent star "Ben" (#1, 1972). It was a sensitive ballad from the future "King of Pop":

> *Ben, the two of us need look no more,*
> *We've both found what we were looking for.*
> *With a friend to call my own, I'll never be alone,*
> *And you, my friend, you'll see,*
> *You've got a friend in me.*

## *Grammatically Challenged Pop* · · · ·

Notwithstanding the Jackson 5's "ABC," grammar has never been the strong suit of rock music. In the '70s, things got significantly worse. For example, in Brownsville Station's juvenile classic "Smokin' in the Boy's Room" (#3, 1973), the possessive

apostrophe on the word "Boy's" was somehow misplaced in the title (the correct spelling was "Boys' Room"). Minus ten points for Brownsville Station.

And then there was Steve Miller, whose "Take the Money and Run" (#11, 1976) was a clear example of why SAT scores were falling faster than Skylab. The story of Billy Joe and Bobby Sue, the two young lovers with nothing better to do, was a grammatical nightmare. First Billy Joe shoots a man while robbing a man's castle and Bobby Sue "took the money and run."

Then Billy Mac, the detective down in Texas ("he knows just exactly what the facts is"), lives off the people's taxes. Texas. Taxes. Facts is. El Paso. Hassle. Castle. That was the sound of your fifth-grade English teacher blowing her head off.

And then there was "The Joker" (#1, 1974). This is the infamous song where Miller speaks of the "pompatus of love." What is the mysterious "pompatus?" This is a question that has ignited debates ever since "The Joker" was released. Don't bother looking it up, you'll only end up feeling . . . pompatus. Whatever that is.

*Steve Miller: He took the money and run.*

# Drugs Are Good For You · · · · · · · ·

Miller's songs were also indicative of another trend—recreational drug use. In "Take the Money and Run," Billy Joe and Bobby Sue like to "get high and watch the tube." In "The Joker," the space cowboy is a smoker and a "midnight toker."

The loosening of the public's attitude toward drugs in the '70s was reflected in these and other pop songs. Musicians quickly discovered that slipping in a reference to drugs helped sell their songs. Titles included "Hooked on a Feeling" by Blue Swede (#1, 1974), "Baby Don't Get Hooked on Me" by Mac Davis (#1, 1972), "Love Is the Drug" by Roxy Music (#30, 1976), and "One Toke Over the Line" by Brewer & Shipley (#10, 1971). And the Doobie Brothers topped them all by naming themselves after a marijuana joint.

These were "High Times." Coke spoons were considered a fashion accessory. Head shops flourished. NORML campaigned for leniency laws for marijuana. Politicians turned a blind eye, and Visine's stock went up, up, up. From Eric Clapton singing "it's alright, it's alright, it's alright, cocaine" to Keith Richards getting busted for heroin in Canada, rock stars contributed to the feeling that everybody was just saying yes.

# Drugs Are Bad For You · · · · · · · · ·

Inevitably, there was a backlash against the celebration of drug use, and a few of these cautionary tales managed to slip on the airwaves, including "King Heroin" (#40, 1972) by James Brown and "That Smell" by former hell-bent boozers Lynyrd Skynyrd. But, for the most part, these warnings fell on deaf ears. When an anti-drug song did enter the Top 40, it usually had all the subtlety of one of those late-period

"Dragnet" episodes where Sgt. Joe Friday blabbers on indignantly to some LSD-addled youth who can only respond with a bleary-eyed "wow."

This was the case with "Once You Understand" (#23, 1972), a quintessential piece of anti-drug hysteria from the 1970s. Released under the name Think, "Once You Understand" remains, to this day, one of the great lost "only in the '70s" moments. The song, if you can even call it that, is really a mini-morality play that intercuts the heated dialogue between a mother and a father and their two wayward children. All the while, one treacly melody keeps repeating the same lyrics: "Things get a little easier once you understand."

The following dialogue gives you some flavor of "Once You Understand":

> *Daughter:* Ma, I'll be home at 11.

> *Mom:* You better be home at 10, or don't bother to come home at all.

> *Father:* When I was your age I was working twelve hours a day, six days a week, helping to pay for the food and the rent.

> *Son:* I don't understand. What's that got to do with me?

> *Father:* If you can't figure that out for yourself, you're stupid.

> *Son:* Hey, Dad, did you see my new guitar? I joined a group.

> *Father:* Son, there's a little bit more to life than joining a group or playing guitar.

> *Son:* Yeah, Dad. What is there to life? Life. Life. Life . . .

# God Rock

The backlash against drugs and, in general, all forms of '70s excess was really no surprise. The very concept of free love and one-night stands, the breakup of the nuclear family, the fallen barriers of censorship—here were all the issues that politicians would be campaigning on for years and decades to come.

One form of the backlash was the burgeoning popularity of religious-based pop (a.k.a., "God rock"). "Doesn't anybody know how to pray?" asked Mark Lindsay in the 1970 hit "Arizona" (#10, 1970). Apparently they did, as evidenced by a preponderance of God rock on the pop charts, including George Harrison's "My Sweet Lord" (#1, 1970), Ocean's "Put Your Hand in the Hand" (#2, 1971), and Sister Janet Mead's "The Lord's Prayer" (#4, 1974).

God rock also made it to the Broadway stage, including "Day By Day" (#13, 1972) from the original cast album of *Godspell* and Helen Reddy's cover of "I Don't Know How to Love Him" (#13, 1971) from Tim Rice and Andrew Lloyd Webber's *Jesus Christ Superstar*.

Suddenly, Jesus was everybody's best friend. "Got to have a friend in Jesus," Norman Greenbaum sang in "Spirit in the Sky" (#3, 1970). "Jesus is Just Alright" (#35, 1973) added the Doobie Brothers. "Won't you look down upon me Jesus, you've got to help me make a stand" asked James Taylor on "Fire and Rain" (#3, 1970).

The peak of God rock occurred when Debby Boone had a smash hit with "You Light Up My Life" (#1, 1977) which spent ten straight weeks at the top of the charts—a feat, incidentally, which qualifies her as the ultimate one-hit wonder since Boone never scored another Top 40 chart hit again.

Who lit up Boone's life? When reporters asked her about the meaning of the song, she told them the inspiration for her torch ballad was her relationship with the Lord and not an actual creature of the flesh.

# Jimmy Carter · · · · · · · · · · · · · · · · · · · · ·

By the time Boone released "You Light Up My Life," the God connection ran all the way to the White House. Jimmy Carter, whose sister Ruth Stapleton was a faith healer, went public with the fact that he was a born-again Christian. Strangely enough after Carter quoted Bob Dylan on the campaign trail, Dylan announced that he had become born again, too.

President Carter personified the '70s in many ways—his fashion sense (denim), his open sexuality ("I have lusted in my heart"), his dysfunctional family (who can forget the sight of a besotted Billy relieving himself on the airport tarmac?), and the fact that he was the first President since the Civil War to come from the South.

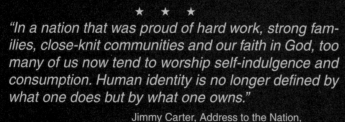

★ ★ ★

*"In a nation that was proud of hard work, strong families, close-knit communities and our faith in God, too many of us now tend to worship self-indulgence and consumption. Human identity is no longer defined by what one does but by what one owns."*

Jimmy Carter, Address to the Nation,
July 15, 1979

★ ★ ★

# Redneck Rock  • • • • • • • • • • • • • • • • •

Carter's ascendancy to the White House allowed a certain amount of long-repressed Southern pride to come to the fore. Until then, the South was considered a place where long hair could get you two rounds with a shotgun á la *Easy Rider* (a fact symbolized by Merle Haggard's infamous anti-hippie rant, "Okie From Muskogee").

But suddenly a bumper crop of bands like the Allman Brothers emerged, sporting Confederate flags and playing hard-rocking R&B and blues. Their rebel yells were typified by the battle cry of Charlie Daniels in "The South's Going to Do It Again" (#29, 1975).

A whole barrel full of bands—Lynyrd Skynyrd, Molly Hatchet, .38 Special, the Marshall Tucker Band, Wet Willie—hit the redneck rocker circuit. Then there was the "outlaw" country of Willie Nelson and Waylon Jennings. Another offshoot of the South rising again was a spate of smash 'em-up, car-chasing movies such as *Smokey and the Bandit*, starring Burt Reynolds and TV shows like "The Dukes of Hazzard."

# CB Radio  • • • • • • • • • • • • • • • • •

There was also a distinctive Southern flavor to the whole CB craze, from the classic laconic drawl of truck drivers muttering "10-4, big buddy" to that twang people instinctively broke into doing their muffled hand-to-the-mouth imitations of a CB transmission.

The CB (or citizens band) radio craze in the mid-'70s was a direct result of strictly enforced 55-mile-per-hour speed limits introduced to conserve gas. Truckers, forced

to use convoys and two-way radios to ward off "the smokeys" (a.k.a., the police), created an entirely new language and culture.

The CB craze finally earned the true stamp of an "only in the '70s" movement with a hit novelty song. It arrived when advertising executive Bill Fries changed his name to C.W. McCall and cut an entertaining quickie about the CB craze called "Convoy" (#1, 1975), which promptly shot to the top of the charts.

# *Kung Fu* · · · · · · · · · · · · · · · · · · · · · · ·

And finally, kung fu. What "only in the '70s" analysis could overlook the classic "Kung Fu Fighting" (#1, 1974) by Carl Douglas? Did it matter that Douglas was a Jamaican singing about the ancient Chinese art? Of course not—this was the '70s!

The climate was ripe for a kung fu hit when Douglas recorded his novelty classic. On TV, David Carradine was playing Kwai Chang Caine, the martial-arts expert with a penchant for Zen philosophy. In the movies, the late, great Bruce Lee was drop-kicking and numb-chucking evil villains in a series of kung fu classics such as *Enter the Dragon*.

Like all great '70s fads, kung fu needed a novelty hit. Ultimately, the honor fell to Douglas, whose insidiously catchy song featured lines like "there were funky Chinamen in funky Chinatown." A few weeks after it was released, "Kung Fu Fighting" zoomed—where else?—straight to number one.

**"FREE BIRD!" "WHIPPING POST!" "LAYLA!" IT'S A ROCK-BLOCK WEEKEND**

*"Hear my song, sing along/Any little song that you know."* –Led Zeppelin, "The Song Remains the Same," 1973

Mega-songs. That's what comes to mind when you recall listening to the radio in the 1970s: songs which went on and on and on . . . and then just kept on going. That was the defining characteristic of a '70s radio behemoth: length.

To this day, it is hard to measure the worth of songs like Led Zeppelin's "Stairway to Heaven" and Lynyrd Skynyrd's "Free Bird" in anything but sheer bulk. Quality, musicianship, innovation—they're all inconsequential. A mega-song was music by the pound.

Back in the '60s, a pithy and concise pop song like "The Letter" took only 1:50 to tell its story. But a mega-song took three times that amount. An instrumental bridge, a verse and a chorus, a few guitar solos and suddenly—poof!—a whole seven minutes had gone by. Like Queen's "Bohemian Rhapsody." Anyone who grew up listening to

*Freddy Mercury of Queen*

FM radio in the '70s, has probably heard this at least 1,000 times—if not more.

Now stop and consider what exactly that means. Each exposure of "Bohemian Rhapsody" is around seven minutes. Multiply by 1,000, and your total exposure comes to 7,000 minutes. Now divide 7,000 by 1,440 (the number of minutes in a day), and you have 4.86. Rounded up, this means you may have spent five days of your life listening to "Bohemian Rhapsody."

Doesn't that make you feel gooooooood?

Songs like "Bohemian Rhapsody" were the kind of epics which came to dominate the FM airwaves in the 1970s. Through endurance, they stretched the limit of the traditional three-minute pop single to the breaking point. But then these were no ordinary songs—they were mega-songs.

What's a mega-song? It is a composition that manages, through endless and insidious repetition, to lodge itself in the collective pop consciousness and stubbornly refuses to leave.

Plus, it is long. Extremely long. This was the strategy of mega-songs: by eating up the airwaves, they assured their place in rock history. Unlike the classic pop single, a mega-song could easily fill up an entire segment of a radio show or an entire side of an album. And that was perfectly all right with the performers who created these songs. More exposure meant more sales. So naturally, musicians began creating longer and longer songs—so long, in fact, that in the time it takes to play the live version of "Free Bird," you can play the "A" side of the first six Beatles singles ("Love Me Do," "Please Please Me," "From Me to You," "She Loves You," "I Want to Hold Your Hand," "Can't Buy Me Love") and still sneak in "Her Majesty."

Where did this madness and insanity start? Although the origins are disputable, the honor could certainly be accorded to Iron Butterfly—a group regarded by many as

*Inna-room-full-of-money: Iron Butterfly goes gold.*

America's first heavy metal band—which in 1968 released a song which lasted seventeen minutes. "In-A-Gadda-Da-Vida" was more than a song—it was sheer mass. The full version of the song, versus the edited single, took up an entire side of an album, during which one solitary riff repeated over and over in a mesmerizing drone. Some people found it interminably boring, others were entranced.

But, in truth, it wasn't the quality of the music that mattered—it was the weight of the experience and, on that account, "In-A-Gadda-Da-Vida" was massive. This was heavy metal at its heaviest, a song which seemingly went on forever (the live version lasted almost twenty minutes) and promised its listeners a trip into the unknown. Once they agreed to enter this mysterious realm of pounding drums and serpentine guitars solos, Iron Butterfly promised they would never have to leave.

And many never did.

The effect of "In-A-Gadda-Da-Vida" was staggering and so were many of the listeners. But that was the appeal of the mega-song—pure escapist pleasure. For ill and for good, Iron Butterfly had proven you could throw everything into the mix and still get played on the radio. And music was never the same. From now on, caution and self-control were thrown to the winds.

Through duration and sheer insouciance, "In-A-Gadda-Da-Vida" had changed the face of music. Compared to this slab of rock, most bands' pithy three-minute pop songs needed a whole lotta heft if they ever hoped to compete on the FM dial.

Thus, the decade of the mega-song was born. Although some may claim the excess and lack of self-control began in the '60s—the group Love, for example, ate up an entire album side of *Da Capo* with the song "Revelation" in 1967—the phenomenon of mega-songs truly came into its own in the '70s.

The mega-song was an everlasting monument to the decade's insatiable thirst for bombast and bluster. Its characteristics—the absurdly grandiose pretensions; the nutty ambition; the complete and utter lack of regard for refinement, taste, and decorum—could well be a description of the '70s itself.

But the songs that typified the mega-song movement were actually quite a diverse lot. Consider the aforementioned selections: "Free Bird" by Lynyrd Skynyrd, "Stairway to Heaven" by Led Zeppelin, and "Bohemian Rhapsody" by Queen. Each is different in approach, tone, and tempo. The only commonality, in fact, is extreme length.

This is a crucial detail. A mega-song wasn't just an extended jam á la Jimi Hendrix or Cream. It was a singular composition with attention paid to

*Lynyrd Skynyrd's guitar army*

detail. Every note was plotted and practiced, and it showed. That is why it is possible to recall the greatest mega-songs note-for-note.

So what songs qualify as mega-songs? Certainly the following have a good claim: "Layla" by Derek and the Dominos, "Whipping Post" by the Allman Brothers, "Won't Get Fooled Again" by The Who, "Smoke on the Water" by Deep Purple, "Don't Fear the Reaper" by Blue Oyster Cult, "Dream On" by Aerosmith, "Roundabout" by Yes, "Hotel California" by the Eagles, "Hold Your Head Up" by Argent, "Do You Feel Like We Do" by Peter Frampton, and "Paradise By the Dashboard Lights" by Meatloaf.

These and other lengthy classics are songs that practically defined the music of the 1970s. Other candidates? Here's a ringer—Pink Floyd's *Dark Side of the Moon*, one mega-song interwoven in a whole mega-album. *Dark Side of the Moon* took the

*Pink Floyd: Somewhere over the rainbow.*

concept of hypnotic songs punctuated by thunderous guitar to the logical extreme. It had all of the qualifications of a mega-song. Specifically, this meant:

1 It sounded good if you were stoned.

2 It was well-produced.

3 It had anthemic aspirations.

4 The lyrics were not too specific.

5 It shifted moods and tempos.

6 It ended in a blaze of guitar pyrotechnics.

7 And last, but not least, it was long.

*Dark Side of the Moon* qualified on all levels—particularly duration, which it delivered in spades. If not for the run-out groove on side "A," it is safe to assume that many listeners would have never snapped out of their stupor.

*Dark Side of the Moon* is a single extended piece rather than a collection of songs. It is a fine album with a textural and conceptual richness that not only invites, but demands involvement. There is a certain grandeur here that exceeds mere musical melodramatics, and is rarely attempted in rock. *Dark Side of the Moon* has flash.
                                        —*Loyd Grossman,* Rolling Stone, *May 24, 1973.*

Of course, there were other mega-albums of the '70s—Boston's eponymous debut comes to mind—but in the final analysis, it is the mega-song that truly defines the 1970s. They emptied lighters and created their own ozone holes and left an indelible impression on the decade as we remember it.

And, yet, categorization is tricky when it comes to the mega-song. Why, for example, can Meat Loaf's pseudo-operatic "Paradise By the Dashboard Lights" be called a mega-song while a '70s standard like Grand Funk's "We're An American Band" does not qualify?

The answer: duration. "Paradise By the Dashboard Lights" took over seven minutes of airtime, making it one of the longest singles ever to hit the Top 40. "We're An American Band," on the other hand, only ate up three minutes and twenty-three seconds. It had everything a mega-song needed except length.

*Edgar Winter*

Many great songs lost out on this technicality alone. For example, being edited for AM radio could disqualify a song. A classic example was Edgar Winter's "Frankenstein." As conceived and originally recorded, "Frankenstein" was a mega-song through and through. It had the shifts, the grooves, the wailing guitars of Ronnie Montrose, the shimmering synthesizer break, the drum solos, and all the excess and abandon that made a mega-song great.

And of course, it had Edgar Winter, a long-haired, cape-wearing albino with a synthesizer slung around his neck, looking like an alien from a distant universe. When it was performed in concert, "Frankenstein" played like a true mega-song. Winter was a whirling dervish, running to and fro, playing drums, saxophones, and walls of synthesizers.

"Frankenstein" was an entire concert in one song. But on the radio, where it was—pardon the pun—a freak hit, the song was pared down to its essence. Reportedly, Winter was so exasperated with the process of editing his as-yet-untitled tour de force for the radio that he named the patched-together version of the original (and superior) free-form version after Mary Shelley's monster.

Like all the best mega-songs, "Frankenstein"—the album version—was flawless in execution and wildly overblown at the same time, giving it that wonderful only-in-the-'70s flavor that flaunted every arena-rock cliche and lodged itself into your gray matter with the efficiency of a steam shovel.

But "Frankenstein," the single, was a different animal altogether, a patchwork of deft edits and stop-on-a-dime pauses. It was also short: three minutes and thirty-five seconds to be exact. And therefore, despite the fact that it is notable in every other respect, you cannot claim, at least in a court of law, that "Frankenstein" is a true mega-song.

What is a true mega-song? If we're looking for a standard, there is only one place to go: "Stairway to Heaven." To this day, Led Zeppelin's signature song continues to define the formula. Upon first exposure, the simple but haunting appeal of the song is due, in large measure, to the intricate guitar work of Jimmy Page and the banshee wailing of Robert Plant.

*Led Zeppelin/Iron Butterfly—coincidence?*

## Words of the '70s

*I could never get along in a band with a pos-turing, posing lead singer.*
—Keith Richards, on Led Zeppelin

\* \* \* \* \* \* \*

However, the real key to "Stairway to Heaven"—and, thus, by association, the real key to any mega-song—is the shifts in tempo and mood. The song begins innocently enough as a light ballad, then settles into a mid-tempo guitar-strummer, revs up to become a furious head-banger, and ends in hushed silence as Plant's quivering vocals trail off into oblivion.

One, two, three, four. It was a magical formula and an effective one, too, as the song's many imitators would soon prove. And yet, despite its external simplicity, "Stairway to Heaven," in many ways, was quite a complex achievement. The trick of the song was that one exposure wasn't enough. After listening to eight minutes of carefully orchestrated moments, many record buyers just picked up the stylus and started the song all over again.

## Slabs of Rock: Length of Some '70s Mega-songs

| SONG | ARTIST | LENGTH |
| --- | --- | --- |
| (Don't Fear) The Reaper | Blue Oyster Cult | 5:08 |
| Smoke on the Water | Deep Purple | 5:42 |
| Hold Your Head Up | Argent | 6:02 |
| Radar Love | Golden Earring | 6:26 |
| Foreplay/Long Time | Boston | 7:32 |
| Stairway to Heaven | Led Zeppelin | 8:00 |
| Life's Been Good | Joe Walsh | 8:04 |
| Paradise by the Dashboard Lights | Meat Loaf | 8:21 |
| Free Bird | Lynyrd Skynyrd | 9:03 |
| Funeral for a Friend/Love Lies Bleeding | Elton John | 11:08 |
| Do You Feel Like We Do (Live) | Peter Frampton | 13:36 |
| Whipping Post | Allman Brothers | 22:52 |

Repetition was the key to the hold of the mega-song. That was the crucial lesson of "Stairway to Heaven." Played once, it was merely long. Played over and over, it began to take over your life. And many people apparently were more than willing to give in, to surrender to the lingering sensation.

A kind of quasi-religious element was implicit in "Stairway to Heaven," albeit an unholy one. Like the sorcerer with the lantern who ruled from the top of the mountain inside the double-gated album sleeve of Led Zeppelin's fourth album, there was a demonic, witching element to this song.

A true mega-song, like a religious order, required devotion and surrender. And once you surrendered to a mega-song, anything could happen. A teenage boy, under its spell, would do anything the performer suggested—sing at the top of his lungs, sway hands, play air guitar, or even imitate his hero's propensity for satanic behavior.

This was the power of the mega-song. It took over your life and became your operating philosophy. You became it, it became you. True fans of "Stairway to Heaven" knew every note by heart. They also knew all of those deliberately obtuse lyrics (and had a habit of carving them into wooden desks in high school).

As poetry, "Stairway to Heaven" was pretty weak stuff. But all of those odd allusions to bustles in hedgerows and May Queens—well, it made you wonder. Cause you know sometimes words have two meanings. Or no meaning at all.

Truthfully, most mega-songs were not about anything at all—they were basically excuses for long guitar solos. "Free Bird" is the classic example. Is it about a bird? Not really. Does it have lots of pyrotechnic guitar solos? For sure.

Actually, the good ol' boys in Lynyrd Skynyrd were clever. By grafting a series of fantastically long guitar solos to a very slight song structure, they masked the song's dirty little secret: "Free Bird" had no chorus. It was just one verse and a bridge. But the group more than made up for these shortcomings with a guitar army of three—count 'em—three guitarists whose extended show-stopping riffing, complete with syncopated triplet harmonies, drove Skynyrd's fans wild.

There was literally no end to the guitar solos on the studio recording of "Free Bird"— like all great mega-songs, it never died, it just faded away. This was another crucial element. A mega-song had to go on forever in the listener's mind. That is how they managed to grow (and grow) and eventually conquer the rock culture of the 1970s, through sheer endurance.

The Allman Brothers' "Whipping Post" is an instructive example of how the legend of the mega-song managed to grow. At first, this forgettable tune appeared to be just another excuse for lead guitarists Duane Allman and Dickie Betts to stretch out.

*The Allman Brothers*

Side four (of *The Allman Brothers Band—At Fillmore East*) is the encore: 22 minutes-plus of Gregg Allman's "Whipping Post," with Duane and Betts trading off leads around Gregg's organ, and both drummers taking off as well—(Butch) Trucks sometimes on timpani. If you've been so unfortunate as to never have caught the Allman Brothers band live, this recording is certainly the next best thing. Turn the volume up all the way and sit through the concert; by the time it's over you can almost imagine the Allman Band getting high and heading back to Macon (where, characteristically they continue to live in unparanoid bliss) on their motor-cycles.

—*George Kimball*, Rolling Stone, *8-19-71*.

Farrrrrrrr out. But to the surprise of everyone, the song became an in-concert phenomenon. During the Allman Brother's performances, fans continued to shout "Whipping Post!" over and over again, like a mantra, in between songs. This presented the band with a curious dilemma—they either had to play "Whipping Post" or leave devoted audiences dissatisfied.

And here, at the foot of "Whipping Post," is the root of all excess. Because now, thanks to its legendary status, every performance of "Whipping Post" had become an act of personal one-upmanship for Allman and Betts. And this, in turn, invited longer and longer flights of guitar.

In essence, this was how the mega-song was born. At its core, there was a sycophantic relationship between needy fans and needy musicians and when it worked, it was magic. When it didn't, it was . . . long.

The kind of long songs that didn't work (think progressive rock) stumbled into the waiting trap of mega-song clichés—noodling guitar solos that meandered into the abyss, pseudo-profound ranting of lead singers who barely graduated from junior high school, and drum solos that crashed and burned ad infinitum.

That's why a truly great mega-song always kept a few tricks up its sleeve. For example, at first glance, Derek and the Dominos' "Layla" seemed to be just another of those airwave-hogging, artery-clogging monsters of FM radio. But after several minutes of furious riffing and anguished singing, "Layla" stopped on a dime. An elegiac piano section began, which lead to an empathetic and virtuostic guitar display by Duane Allman and Eric Clapton.

This ingenuous turnaround had a calming effect, a rare commodity indeed for a mega-song. The long, lovely fade allowed Allman's shimmering slide guitar solo to

transport listeners to places they never dreamed a mega-song could go.

"Layla" is also a perfect example of the inter-connectivity among all of the great mega-songs. Like one glorious block of rock, each one is inseparable from the others.

For example, Eric Clapton ("Layla") and Jimmy Page ("Stairway to Heaven") both started their careers as members of the British blues band the Yardbirds. Likewise, it was Clapton who invited Duane Allman to join Derek and the Dominos after hearing his work on "Whipping Post."

The connections keep mounting. For example, Allman's death in a motorcycle accident inspired Lynyrd Skynyrd to dedicate "Free Bird" in his honor. And in 1977, Ronnie Van Zant and Steve Gaines of Lynyrd Skynyrd died in a plane crash. Spooky.

Death was a major theme in mega-songs. The Grim Reaper made morbid cameos on "Whipping Post" ("Oh, Lord, I feel like I'm dying"), "Bohemian Rhapsody" ("Mama, I just killed a man"), Elton John's "Funeral for

Eric Clapton

125

a Friend/Love Lies Bleeding" ("It kills me to think of you with another man")—not to mention, the obvious "(Don't Fear) The Reaper" and "Stairway to Heaven."

But death was only one theme. If you rated all of the mega-song's different themes in terms of importance it would go something like this: sex, death, and fire.

Fire played a crucial role when mega-songs were performed—most noticeably, when the sea of lighters ritualistically lit up the rock arenas during mega-song encores. It is also represented by "Smoke on the Water," a mega-smash for Deep Purple in 1973 and a seminal example of the form.

\* \* \* \* \* \* \*

## Words of the '70s

*Our main audience is about eighteen years old. People that age don't really understand music that much. . . . If they were really that musically hip, they wouldn't even like us.*
—Ritchie Blackmore, Deep Purple

\* \* \* \* \* \* \*

Sex, however, is the most dominant theme of the mega-song. Length. Duration. The maximum amount of pleasure. Sex was implicit in the very structure of the average mega-song.

The average sex act, according to the Kinsey Report, lasted seven minutes. So did the mega-song. But the similarities did not end there. In every mega-song, a climax was implied. In concert the last note was held for an unendurably long time as drums crashed, guitar picks scraped, and the light show operator maniacally pushed all of the special effects buttons. Finally, it was over. "Sioux City—you've been great," the

The **RHINO** History of Rock 'n' Roll

*Heart*

lead singer would say, withdrawing into the darkness and moving on to the next one-night stand. Tension and release were the central dynamics at work in every great mega-song. Whether it was the pent-up frustration of "Layla" ("you've got me on me knees"), or the ecstatic release of Neil Young's "Like a Hurricane" ("I'm getting blown away"), the mega-song promised transcendence in the end.

Sex, death, and fire, it just so happens, are the main preoccupations of the average fifteen-year-old boy. By embracing a teenager's perspective on the world (sex, sex, cars, guitars, sex, and more sex) the mega-song gave sustenance to those who sought to nurture the eternal fifteen-year-old boy within.

For many of us in our cavity-prone years, the availability of sex was summed up by Steven Tyler: "Dream On." But by its very nature, the mega-song invited autoerotic pleasures like air guitar with its rhythmic stroking near the region of the groin.

It just so happens that the physics of air guitar seemed better suited to males. In general, so was the entire mega-song phenomenon. The only female performers of note were the Wilson sisters of Heart who scored mega-songs hits with "Barracuda" and "Magic Man."

One thing that both sexes could share, however, was the illicit sensations that the mega-song invited. "Let's get high a while," sang the Wilson sisters on "Magic Man," and many people, both male and female, took them up on it.

Drugs opened the doors of perception to the pleasures of a mega-song. If everything worked properly, the mood would envelop you, connecting you to an unseen community of likeminded individuals. The drug of choice? Unquestionably, it was pot. Marijuana invited narcissistic, inward-gazing behavior that was conducive to the enjoyment of a mega-song. Leaning back on some pillows, staring at the black-light poster in your bedroom, and listening to a mega-song on your headphones—in a nutshell, that was nirvana in the 1970s.

There was the holy water of the bong, the smoking technique, which required a long inhalation of air with a finger strategically placed over the carborator and then there was inevitable paroxysms after inhaling too much smoke. The whole thing smacked of some Dada-esque version of Eastern hookah smoking rituals. But it was more than a feeling—fans of mega-songs couldn't be satisfied with one hit. Their appetite was insatiable. Like addicts, they called radio stations and demanded their fix.

There was an unwritten rule about the mega-song. Once a song was in the pantheon, it could not be removed. The cosmic playlist would not allow it. In this way, the DJs

were at one with their audience. DJs wanted to play the songs, the audience wanted to hear them. For disc jockeys, the mega-song amounted to extended coffee breaks. They could put on "Free Bird," send out for Chinese, pop open a beer, kick their legs up on the console, and take requests from listeners (more mega-songs, of course).

Since a real mega-song ate up at least seven minutes of airtime, DJs had plenty of time to ponder their next choice. Would it be "Won't Get Fooled Again" or "Hotel California?" Why choose? You could play them both and drive over to the 7-Eleven for a Slurpee.

Listeners kept demanding their mega-songs, and radio stations kept playing them. And that's an important point—without those devoted listeners, mega-songs would have been nothing more than a bunch of very long songs. But through the willing participation of musicians, DJs, radio station programmers, record labels, and listeners, the mega-song became something bigger than itself.

"Free Bird" is a perfect example. Somewhere in the universe, "Free Bird" has been playing continuously since the 1970s. During that time, it has become almost a metaphysical presence in our lives. Over and over, "Free Bird" repeats, its ions traversing the radio spectrum, blanketing the airwaves with its unique pattern of pitch and melody, making contact with car antennas and bursting forth out over our car speakers.

Locked in this endlessly repeating cycle, "Free Bird" has become more than the sum of its parts, more than a bunch of rowdy Confederate rock fans dry-heaving Jack Daniels into stadium toilets, more than a thousand teenage boys playing air guitar in front of a mirror. "Free Bird" has become a living organism, a force unto itself.

In a sense, "Free Bird" existed forever. The musicians of Lynyrd Skynyrd simply plucked the notes out of the troposphere, assembled them into a neat epigrammatic line, sorted the good notes, tossed out the bad, and put the song together in the way that the rock gods of the mega-song had fashioned.

In other words, it was fate. And so, too, was the unlucky destiny of Ronnie Van Zandt and the others who perished in that terrible plane crash. Is it too much of an exaggeration to say the great wave of mega-songs came to an end with the death of Van Zandt? Certainly, no great mega-song of note was recorded after this unfortunate tragedy.

But I have a confession to make here. The day after the Skynyrd plane crash, there was this girl sitting next to me in math class who was really broken up, and being a callow teenager, I thought she was being a little melodramatic about it all. I remember thinking, "It isn't like John Lennon got shot or something."

And, now, I see why she was so upset. "Free Bird" touched the hearts of those willing to partake in its received wisdom and perhaps Lennon, himself, was listening; after all, he did write a song called "Free as a Bird." In their own modest way, the members of Lynyrd Skynyrd were attempting to satisfy its audience's longings for immortality. As musicians, they were merely shamans who could conjure up the collective unconscious urges of their faithful audiences—the urge to play forever. And they ended up creating a song which, like primordial DNA in an endless spiral, just kept replicating itself until it evolved into something bigger than itself—something that would outlive not only the people who played it but the people who listened to it.

Through duration comes transcendence. That is the lesson of the mega-song. And likewise, through death comes regeneration. And so on and so forth.

It gets pretty philosophical when you start to consider all of the implications of the mega-song. For example, what happens to a song which is played a billion times? Does it change in any metaphysical way? Is it possible to hear a song differently once

it has been heard a billion times? The mega-song invites a whole host of questions like these. But the answers don't come as easily.

Perhaps the closest anyone ever came was the group Boston. Half-way through their seven-plus minute opus "Foreplay/Long Time," their lead singer Brad Delp sang "it's been such a long time." And, really, what more could you say?

*On "Long Time," Boston delivered everything they promised . . . and more.*

# BAD GIRLS, GOOD TIMES, FREAK OUT!

*"Do it."* –Van McCoy, "The Hustle," 1975

Disco was the great divide in the '70s. You either loved it or hated it, and you had to take a stand either way. That stand could say so much about you—about your musical preferences, your fashion choices, the way you liked to dance, even your attitudes about sex.

There was no in-between about disco. Some people thought it was monotonous, insipid, offensive, even threatening. Yet others reveled in it, made love to it, and gladly grabbed all of the uninhibited pleasures it promised.

Looking back on it twenty years later, it's difficult to see what the fuss was about— the music world didn't crumble as some rock faithful feared, and eventually, like all pop crazes, disco fizzled out.

Now that the dust has settled—to the point where even the most unregenerate disco hater can admit that "Stayin' Alive" is a pretty catchy song—it is time to address the basic misperceptions that have dominated the discussion of disco ever since its emergence in the 1970s.

Rather than spend an entire book trying to squeeze every last bit of significance out of John Travolta's white three-piece suit (i.e. "Deconstructing the Mirror Ball: The Rise and Fall of *Saturday Night Fever* as Cultural Artifact"), we will limit our discussion to the five following points. If everything goes smoothly, like the orchestrated moves of "The Hustle," you can glide through the process painlessly.

*1* Disco and sex were inextricably linked. You cannot discuss the former without discussing the latter.

*2* Disco did not exist in a vacuum. Other social movements contributed to its rise and fall as a cultural force.

*3* The music of disco was not only under-appreciated but generally misunderstood.

*4* It is doubtful we will see the likes of disco again. It was a once-in-a-lifetime event.

*5* And the last point—and perhaps the most disputable—disco didn't suck. No, really, we're serious.

The first point—that sex and disco were virtually interchangeable—needs little elaboration. The producers, songwriters, and performers who created disco did little to cover up the fact that sexual pleasure was the driving force of the music. This was evident from the earliest days of disco. "TSOP" by MSFB, one of the first songs to popularize the genre, had only nine words in the entire song: "Let's get it on, it's time to get down." But what else was there to say? Disco was about sex. End of story.

The thump thump thump thump of the bass drum told you all you needed to know. The dance groove was so sexually suggestive that it could only be interpreted as a simulation of the act itself. Unlike rock 'n' roll, where the musicians were the objects of carnal desire, dancers were the main attraction in disco. On Sister Sledge's "He's the Greatest Dancer," the "champion of dance" is so desirable that "he never leaves the disco alone."

More than the music, dancing was the clearest expression of disco's sexuality. Judging from the millions willing to join in, the effect was positively libidinous. "My body needs action," sang Shirley and Company's Shirley Goodman on "Shame, Shame, Shame," adding a sassy "so get out of my way."

Disco spoke of new sexual possibilities and confidence. The shame was on you, Shirley sang, if you couldn't join in the fantasy. This was uncharted territory: sex without boundaries. The "Adonis" on the dance floor in "He's the Greatest Dancer" is quite obviously familiar with one-night stands. The singer at the disco issues her come-on without hesitation: "Please take me home."

Both "He's the Greatest Dancer" and "Shame, Shame, Shame" were open and unabashed expressions of female desire. Traditionally in pop music, women had been relegated to the role of sexual prey. In disco, they were finally the predators, their desires fully acknowledged.

*Diana Ross*

More than an expression of unrepentant sexuality, disco announced a radical shift of gender roles in popular entertainment. And that brings us to the second point: Disco did not exist in a vacuum. To explain away these wholesale changes in society's attitude toward sex, you must first consider the implications and significance of movements such as the drive for women's rights in the 1970s.

Feminism was a silent but key component in the emergence of disco. The fight to establish women's rights to control their own bodies was an essential factor both in the sexual revolution and the rise of disco as a cultural force. The popular acceptance of the sexuality of disco divas such as Diana Ross and Donna Summer was one of the first signs that men and women were on equal footing when it came to expressing their physical needs.

Other forces were at work as well. Various forms of contraception added to the opportunities for experimental sex. People pushed the boundaries of sexual expression—in fashion (skin-tight lycra pants for women, gold chains and unbuttoned polyester shirts for men), in fragrances (patchouli oil for women, musk for men), in books (*The Joy of Sex*), in underground clubs (The Crisco Disco), in hot tubs, in water beds, in *flagrante delicto*.

The pent-up tension of sexual repression resulted in the wildest expression of sexual energy in modern history—a frenzy of impulsive desire. There was a sense, out there on the multicolored disco dance floor, that you better get it while you can, before conservative America put the kibosh on the whole thing.

Some people took that mission to heart particularly, but not exclusively, the gay community which, sexually, had felt the shackles as much, if not more, than anybody else. Their newly acquired sexual emancipation was also a major factor in the emergence of disco. It was in underground gay clubs where disco first found its voice. The Village People, in particular, brought gay archetypes to the masses—even if the subtexts of songs like "Macho Man" were sufficiently blurred.

The exuberance of the disco phenomenon was, in many ways, a celebration that marked a great coming-out party for the gay community—certainly, it was a signifier that announced they could no longer be ignored. When Sylvester, the first successful openly gay performer sang "You Make Me Feel (Mighty Real)," it was a milestone both culturally and politically. The two could not be separated when it came to establishing the gay community as a visible force in society.

Identity was an all-important factor in disco. But roles—racial, gender, sexual—were deliberately obscured. Participants were not limited to identifiable labels like gay, straight, male, or female. Disco diva Grace Jones sang that she felt like a woman but

## Songs With the Word "Boogie" in the Title

**1970**
"Full-Tilt Boogie"
- *Janis Joplin*

**1973**
"Boogie Woogie Bugle Boy"
- *Bette Midler*

**1974**
"Boogie Down"
- *Eddie Kendricks*
"Jungle Boogie"
- *Kool & The Gang*
"Steppin' Out (Gonna Boogie Tonight)"
- *Dawn*

**1975**
"Bertha Butt Boogie (Part 1)"
- *Jimmy Castor Bunch*
"Boogie On Reggae Woman"
- *Stevie Wonder*

**1976**
"Boogie Fever"
- *Sylvers*
"Get Up and Boogie"
- *Silver Convention*

**1977**
"Boogie Child"
- *The Bee Gees*
"Boogie Nights"
- *Heatwave*
"Boogie 'Til You Puke"
- *Root Boy Slim and the Sex Change Band*
"I'm Your Boogie Man"
- *KC & The Sunshine Band*

**1978**
"Boogie Oogie Oogie"
- *Taste of Honey*
"Boogie Shoes"
- *KC & The Sunshine Band*

**1979**
"Boogie Wonderland"
- *Earth, Wind & Fire with the Emotions*
"Boogie Motion"
- *Beautiful Bend*
"Boogie Woogie Dancin' Shoes"
- *Claudja Barry*
"Mindless Boogie"
- *Hot Chocolate*

looked like a man, and she was accepted for who she was—a divine creature in a rarified state of the world.

Attitude was everything—in disco music, in disco clubs, and out on the dance floor—and personal identity surrendered to the beat. "Let your mind and your body be free," sang Peter Brown on "Dance with Me"—this may have been the most radical concept of the entire disco movement. Free minds, free bodies. It is not surprising that some people found that notion threatening.

But again, disco did not exist in a vacuum. There was a sexual revolution going on. And some of the sex, like a lot of the music, was anonymous. It didn't matter who you were dancing with or what you were dancing to, the point was to lose yourself in a sea of mutual gratification.

This set of circumstances lead to a primary criticism of disco: it was shallow. There was no subtlety to the seduction. The only question was, "Your place or mine?" Or, to use a catch-phrase from a later era, "What's love got to do with it?"

From outward appearances, very little. In disco, love, like identity, surrendered to the rhythm. As a result, disco was seen as emotionally deficient. Like the synthesizers that created the metronomic beat, it lacked heart. Or, at least, so said its detractors.

This brings us to the third point—that disco was grossly misunderstood. In reality, beneath the glitter and glamour, there was a lot of heartbreak in the lyrical content. Classic disco songs like "Don't Leave Me This Way" by Thelma Houston and "I Will Survive" by Gloria Gaynor spoke about the pain of love rather than the joy of sex.

*Gloria Gaynor*

Perhaps the greatest summation of the emptiness that accompanied the insatiable sexual quest of disco was Inner Life's "I'm Caught Up (In A One Night Love Affair)." Listeners learned of an anguished woman who keeps inviting anonymous men back to her home. The singer acknowledges, in the middle of her latest encounter, that she does not expect to find love, telling her current suitor that "tomorrow you'll be on your way." After inviting the anonymous man to make himself at home, she implores him not to say anything about love or to make any promises. Although their sexual encounter is imminent, there is no joy or elation in her words, only a sense of quiet desperation:

> *I haven't got much time*
>
> *To find the man behind the smile.*
>
> *I'm a fairy tale princess*
>
> *In search of a knight*
>
> *And I never believed dreams come true.*
>
> *I'm just like you.*

As the song continues, the singer's voice becomes increasingly strained. She's in control but also out of control as she guides the man through the motions. "Close the door and I'll get next to you. . . . Just what are we going to do?"

There's no question that the physical act will be consummated. The only mystery is whether they can find something more substantial. The title of the song "I'm Caught Up" suggests that this is a tale of sexual addiction. But the truth comes out—she's

still holding on to a strand of hope that somehow in her frequent encounters, "true love will find her there."

There was much emotion in disco—mainly jealousy, defiance, and the will to survive. But too often the music of disco did not reflect the reality—free sex did not guarantee real love. Physical pleasure superseded any notion of romance. There was no definitive corollary between the brief physical act and something more permanent in people's lives.

Disco generally acknowledged that love was fleeting. In the end, the fantasy of disco involved losing yourself in the moment, escaping the mundane aspects of your life, transporting yourself to other places, other realities. In other words, it was a lot like an episode of "The Love Boat."

*The Love Boat*

Yes, that long-running soap opera on the sea, by some cosmic coincidence, seemed to parallel the rise and fall of disco—debuting in 1977, the same year Studio 54 hit Manhattan, and going off the air in 1985, the year it was announced that Rock Hudson had AIDS. But the true link between "The Love Boat" and disco is the show's theme. Sung with leering aplomb by Jack Jones, it sums up all of disco's unrequited promises in one pithy TV theme song:

> Love, exciting and new,
>
> Come aboard, we're expecting you.
>
> Love, life's sweetest reward,
>
> Let it flow, it flows back to you.
>
> The Love Boat
>
> Soon will be making another run.
>
> The Love Boat
>
> Promises something for everyone.

The key phrase was the line "love won't hurt anymore." That was the one promise that disco could not deliver. Each week's episode aboard the *Pacific Princess* might spark a new romance but romance is fleeting. In the end, like disco, "Love Boat" was only a temporary escape, one hour of fantasy island, before it was time to go back to the land of bland reality.

Disco's legion of disgruntled naysayers often saw the music as a low-rent bump-and-grind, straight out of Vegas, all glamour and glitz and t-and-a. Granted, disco was sensual and its lyrics veered toward various explicit ways of describing sex. The song titles were a dead give-away of their intent: "It Only Takes a Minute Girl," "More, More, More," "Give It Up," "Ring My Bell," "Get Down Tonight," "In the Bush," "How Deep is Your Love," "Get Off," "Kiss You All Over," "You Sexy Thing," and "Do Ya Think I'm Sexy?"

But disco hardly invented the idea of sex and music—it just exploited it. Besides, plenty of songs in every genre of the '70s matched the lascivious intensity of disco. "Jungle Fever," a 1972 smash hit by the Belgian group Chakachas was about as erotic as any pop song that ever slipped into *Billboard*'s Top Ten before or after disco. Its explicit moans and sighs pushed the boundaries of good taste as far as Donna Summer's orgasmic ecstasy did on "Love to Love You Baby" three years later.

And this leads us back to point three: disco music was grossly misunderstood. The true stylistic innovation of disco was not a simulation of sex through suggestive lyrics but the simulation of rhythm through synthesizers. Rhythm was the dominant element. Everything came down to a beat which stimulated dancing and created the hypnotic pulse which kept the crowds in constant motion and sway. Dancers were, in essence, slaves to the rhythm. As Grace Jones sang:

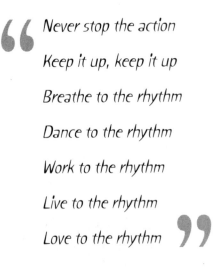

*Never stop the action*

*Keep it up, keep it up*

*Breathe to the rhythm*

*Dance to the rhythm*

*Work to the rhythm*

*Live to the rhythm*

*Love to the rhythm*

The introduction of drum machines aided and abetted the creation of the rhythm immeasurably. The formula of disco music required a certain amount of beats per minute and, with the benefit of these new high-tech machines, an anonymous music producer working with anonymous studio musicians could create a dance track with little effort.

The drum machine's mathematical precision may have removed some of the spontaneity from the music but it also added the mechanical drive which became disco's hallmark. This inevitably led to the accusation that disco was an utterly synthetic creation, bereft of melody and innovation and an affront to the finely tuned Top 40 pop sensibilities of the American public.

This might have been the biggest lie about disco. Not only were dozens of songs memorable and melodic but, among those pearls, a variety of sounds were introduced: a solidarity sing-a-long "We Are Family" by Sister Sledge, a futuristic rendering of Richard Strauss' "Also Sprach Zarathustra (2001)" by Deodato, the sly and cutting humor of "Heart of Glass" by Blondie and the cold and robotic techno-groove of "1 Feel Love" by Donna Summer.

*Donna Summer on the radio*

The two latter compositions, which were produced by the original svengali of disco, Giorgio Moroder, fused the atmospherics of synth-rockers like Kraftwerk to the sounds of American soul music and forged a radical synthesis which continues to influence dance music today.

Two other distinctive producers were Bernard Edwards and Nile Rodgers. What Sam Phillips was to the Sun sound, what Phil Spector was to the Wall of Sound, what George Martin was to the Beatles, Edwards and Rodgers were to disco. They were triple threats—players (Edwards on bass, Rodgers on guitar), producers, and writers.

Rodgers and Edwards produced a warm but insistent brand of dance which never surrendered pop values to repetitive synth beats. As members of Chic, they not only gave disco two of its most distinctive hits, "Le Freak" and "Good Times," but laid bare the lie that disco was overly synthetic. Rodgers, in particular, was a brilliant rhythm guitar player—his elegant but economical guitar parts were living proof that guitars and disco could peacefully co-exist in the same song.

The anonymous violins of "Fly, Robin, Fly" and other early disco hits played a large role in alienating the hardcore rock contingent. For many, the greatest apostasy of disco as music were those long instrumental breaks without a guitar solo.

---

### The Top 10 Singles of 1979

| | |
|---|---|
| 1. "My Sharona" - The Knack | 6. "Reunited" - Peaches & Herb |
| 2. "Le Freak" - Chic | 7. "Ring My Bell" - Anita Ward |
| 3. "Do Ya Think I'm Sexy?" - Rod Stewart | 8. "I Will Survive" - Gloria Gaynor |
| 4. "Bad Girls" - Donna Summer | 9. "Too Much Heaven" - Bee Gees |
| 5. "YMCA" - Village People | 10. "Hot Stuff" - Donna Summer |

A violin, to rockers, was the farthest string instrument away from their beloved guitar—it just couldn't be plugged into a Marshall stack or smashed with the same efficiency.

Where were the power chords? Rockers didn't wait for the answer, they just switched the radio station. And then, much to their annoyance, they would hear some disco trend-jumper like Mick Jagger performing "Miss You." Disco sell-outs were a dime a dozen. Probably the most famous example of rocker going disco occurred in 1978 when Rod Stewart had an international smash with the ludicrously titled "Do Ya Think I'm Sexy?" But at least Stewart made it up to the world by donating the royalties to UNICEF.

In truth, if rockers were looking for a power-chord fix they could have just as easily turned to the opening chords to Donna Summer's 1979 chart-topper "Hot Stuff." Sounding more like Bad Company than "Bad Girls," it even had guitar solos, not to mention Summer's tough rock chick vocals ("sitting here eating my heart out baby"). It rocked with authority.

But by that time it was too late. So many unspeakable crimes had been committed in the name of disco that its reputation was beyond repair. Of course, no one could force disgruntled rockers to buy a disco record and so many never did. And, by the same token, no one could force them, if they despised the idea of dancing at the local discotheque, to enter the premises and, likewise, many never did.

However, by making these choices, the people who scorned disco missed out on experiencing one of the most unique dance phenomenons of the 20th century or, for that matter, of all time. And that brings us to the fourth point: that disco, as a phenomenon, will never be repeated. This can be stated with assurance because the events which came to characterize the disco movement—the anonymous sexual

*The icon of disco—John Travolta as Tony Manero*

The RHINO History of
Rock 'n' Roll

encounters, the liberal use of mind-altering substances, the wild and often-bizarre synthetic fashions, the celebrity cachet of Studio 54—can never possibly re-emerge simultaneously.

The brilliance of disco was in the fleeting nature of the moment. Like a thousand points of light refracted off a mirror ball, everybody was a superstar on the disco dance floor for as long as the beat continued. And when the "Last Dance" was over, so was everyone's fifteen minutes of fame, just as Andy Warhol—the doyen of disco—had predicted.

In fact, looking back on the ever-so-brief rise and fall of disco, it has all the earmarks of a classic Warhol prank: ephemeral moments of celebrity, instant superstars, glamour and glitz, lurid voyeuristic appeal, and, not least, a giddy sense of artificial buoyancy.

The Warholesque quality of disco—particularly the aspect of fleeting fame—reached its apotheosis in John Travolta's riveting performance as dancer Tony Manero in the smash-hit movie *Saturday Night Fever*. The appeal of the movie was simple. Manero was everyman, a working stiff during the day, a nobody. But, at night, out on the disco dance floor, he was a superstar straight out of Warhol's Factory.

The lesson of the movie was that Manero's fantasy existence, as played out at his local disco, was as much of a dead-end in terms of his personal life as his job at a paint store was in terms of his career ambitions. But, typical of the disco phenomenon, people preferred to see the glamour, not the frustration and futility of his endeavors.

The scenes of Travolta dressing for his big night out, smoothing his hair and preening in front of a mirror, captured the true essence of disco. This reflected the fantasy that you could transform yourself in front of your own eyes. Provided you could afford the clothes and master the dance moves, you could reinvent yourself, like Tony Manero, and have your 125-beats-per-minute of fame.

The glamour of disco—or the delusion of disco, depending on your point of view— was that with the right attitude, the right dance moves, and the right fashion accessories, nothing could hold you back from getting a piece of the action. It didn't matter if you were black, white, straight, gay, urban, suburban, a celebrity or a nobody. Everybody was welcome to give it a whirl on the dance floor.

In theory. Actually, everybody was invited to give it a whirl provided the price of admission was paid. That's why the working-class roots of Tony Manero in *Saturday Night Fever*, although endearing as a dramatic device, were based on a false premise. Disco required money and status.

The bitter truth was just a velvet rope away. At the most select discos, like Studio 54, screeners chose a lucky few who got into the party. You might get in on looks, if you were one of the beautiful people; you might get in because you were a great dancer; but you were absolutely sure to get in if you had enough money or celebrity stature.

The fact that Studio 54 became internationally famous had nothing to do with the Tony Maneros of the world. It was celebrities such as Truman Capote, Jackie Onassis, Liza Minelli, and, of course, Andy Warhol who lent the movement its allure. Although they might deny it, a lot of people came to Studio 54 to bask in reflected glory.

It was chic, it was glamorous, it was exclusive. And, inevitably, for many people, it was alienating as well. Beyond those velvet ropes, there was a sense of priviledge which rubbed the less fortunate the wrong way. When a ten-dollar pair of blue jeans suddenly cost ten times that amount because they sported a designer's name, many

*Andy Warhol with Socialite Cornelia Guest and Truman Capote at NYC's Xenon Disco.*

figured disco had become too big for its own britches.

Meanwhile, a disco backlash was taking hold—a backlash which was so forceful and effective that being tagged a disco artist was soon to become the musical equivalent of being called soft on Communism during the McCarthy years.

The backlash began with the catch-phrase "disco sucks" and culminated in a riot. But, almost from the beginning, a tidal wave of resentment had been building. Some people resented the fact that you had to get dressed up to go to a disco. You didn't need to look in the mirror before going to a rock concert. Other people resented the fact that the dances required learning choreography and taking lessons. You didn't need lessons to dance at a rock concert.

Also, there was also a threatening element to free sex, especially if the atomic blow-dried dirt-bag down the hall was getting all of the action while you were home alone. And then there were the gay connotations. The fact that disco allowed gay men to gather in groups and become visible as a community upset the sensibilities of conservative Americans. They saw Sodom and Gomorrah in the blatant eroticism of the music and, more to the point, the unapologetic promiscuity it seemed to inspire.

Long before the "angry white male" was isolated by political pollsters, it was plainly evident that anybody who sported a "disco sucks" bumpersticker or who sang along with gusto to Bob Seger's "Old Time Rock 'n' Roll" was not going to be a candidate to "get down tonight" and "shake his booty."

But the degree of resentment felt towards disco was not fully understood until the riot in 1979. Every phenomenon must have a defining event, the one epochal moment when the spirit of a cultural movement is distorted beyond all recognition and crushed, a moment from which it can never recover.

If the '60s had Altamont to expose the dark underbelly of the Woodstock Dream, the '70s had the disco riot on July 12, 1979; one frightful evening in Chicago where all of the anger and fear associated with disco exploded in a hate-filled expression of rage.

That night a Chicago DJ decided to blow up a box full of disco records as a publicity stunt between games of a baseball doubleheader at Comiskey Park. As soon as

Steve Dahl set the records on fire, thousands of drunken fans, chanting "Disco sucks! Disco sucks!" trashed the ballpark until baton-swinging cops were called in to quell the rioting crowd.

Rioting over what? Music. A simple little beat. But the anti-disco hordes weren't going to stand for passive resistance anymore. This music had to be burned. The entire phenomenon was too powerful and threatening. It needed to be snuffed.

And wouldn't you know it, within a year disco was dead. A combination of events sealed its fate: Steve Rubell and Ian Schrager, the owners of Studio 54, were arrested and sent to jail for income tax evasion. Two million dollars were spent on a disco musical called "Got Tu Go Disco" which bombed on Broadway in 1979. David Berkowitz—a.k.a., the "Son of Sam"—went on a killing spree, specifically targeting young couples coming out of disco clubs. And radio stations started advertising "Bee Gee Free" weekends.

The writing was on the wall. And, to be fair, the spontaneity of disco, as music, was running dry. The songs became formulaic. Without any innovative new stars, the music began to lack inspiration. Just the same beat over and over again.

By the early '80s, for all intents and purposes, the original disco scene—the incandescent one of Studio 54 and the Copacabana—was moribund. Its apocalyptic end had been foreshadowed in 1978 on the Trammps' classic "Disco Inferno" whose "burn, baby, burn" provided a perfect musical commentary on the dying embers of a flame which had once burned so brightly.

Disco was dead. Long live disco.

And that brings us to the last point—whether or not disco really sucks. Not sucked, as in past tense, but sucks. Because, in reality, disco never really died. People never stopped

*Like a diva—Madonna*

dancing to disco beats, they just changed the name to techno, hip hop, house, jungle, ambient, electronica or, simply, dance music.

Madonna? Her early records certainly sound like disco. They were produced, after all, by Chic's Nile Rodgers. And in her wanton ways, she seems to carry on the tradition of a disco diva who emanates sexual desire. But Madonna is not considered a disco artist. She is just an artist.

The word disco is dead, joining the graveyard of '70s lexicon along with "keep on truckin'," "I'm OK, You're OK," "10-4 good buddy," and "what's your sign?" It is a dodo bird—a word which is extinct for any functional purpose beyond memory. Call it what you will, just don't call it disco. That's the mantra.

And, in the final analysis, disco really was just a label. What you read into it said more about you than the label itself. As for whether disco sucked, that was also up to you. Maybe it was liberating, maybe it was the drumbeat of barbarians—it all depended on your point of view.

The beat goes on. It can be found all over the world, anywhere a crowd is locked into a metronomic rhythm. Somewhere out there lost on the dance floor, in the scattered synapses of the strobe light, the true message of disco can be heard in the well-chosen words of Bernard Edwards and Nile Rodgers on Chic's "Everybody Dance." This is disco's promise:

> *Music never lets you down*
>
> *Puts a smile on your face . . .*
>
> *Dancing helps you leave the pain,*
>
> *Soothes your mind,*
>
> *Makes you happy again.*
>
> *Listen to those dancing beats,*
>
> *Close your eyes and let go.*

# THE END OF THE '70s

*"It's the end, the end of the '70s. It's the end, the end of the century."*
—The Ramones, "End of the Century," 1980

The year 1979 turned out be particularly significant, filled with omens that the music world would never be the same. Among the notable events were the overdose death of ex-Sex Pistol bass player Sid Vicious, the disbandment of Led Zeppelin after the death of drummer John Bonham, and an anti-disco rally that turned ugly, resulting in hundreds of arrests in Chicago.

There were also a couple of bright notes. A newcomer named Prince made his debut and Michael Jackson's solo career received a boost with the release of his outstanding dance album *Off the Wall.* In the world of classic rock, Pink Floyd won critical praise and mass success with *The Wall* and both the Police ("Roxanne") and the Knack ("My Sharona") scored breakthrough hits in new wave.

But in the waning months of 1979 it was already clear the music industry would never be the same. More than any other song, "Video Killed the Radio Star" by the Buggles captured the unmistakable feeling that an epoch was ending. Released in late 1979, the song proved to be prescient in several different ways.

First, as an early example of '80s-styled techno-pop, "Video Killed the Radio Star" was emblematic of the new sounds that emphasized synthesizers rather than guitars. Second, the song's title and its subject matter, coming before the tidal wave of video bands, foreshadowed the influence of MTV and the changes in the way music would be made and marketed.

Like television, which had wiped out an entire class of radio performers who relied on their voice rather than their appearance, videos would radically shift the nature of the music business. "We can't rewind," the song's lyrics warned, "we've gone too far." And, indeed, as the events to follow would demonstrate, there was no going back—particularly to the 1970s.

The Buggles hit was a self-fulfilling prophecy. All you had to do was substitute the words "'70s rock star" for "radio star" and basically, you had the artistic dilemma that musicians now faced: Either create a marketable image for yourself or perish.

At 12:01 A.M. on August 1, 1981, nearly two years after the Buggles released their solitary hit, MTV inaugurated its service with "Video Killed the Radio Star." It was an apt choice. Symbolically, the introduction of an all-music network that emphasized pre-recorded clips over live performances meant an important aspect of the 1970's music scene had come to an end.

The programming of music videos in constant rotation meant a shift away from the participatory nature of rock in the '70s to the passive observation of the 1980s.

The **RHINO** History of Rock 'n' Roll

Songs would no longer be judged on their musical merits alone—musicians would need a video to even hope for a hit.

MTV became the definitive way to sell records in the 1980s. And significantly, very few musicians who were associated with the '70s—the major exceptions being Michael Jackson and a few left-field successes like Aerosmith and ZZ Top—managed to make the tricky transition from rock star to video star. "Pictures came and broke your heart," as the Buggles sang. "Put all the blame on VCR."

Radio was also undergoing a demographic shift. By the early '80s, the format known as album-oriented rock (AOR) was already in the process of becoming an oldies rotation. No longer tolerant of new sounds, particularly the sound of synthesizers, AOR programmers narrowed their focus to a few classic rock songs. AOR became the elephant burial ground for the bands of the '70s—Led Zeppelin, Pink Floyd, Lynyrd Skynyrd, Deep Purple, Boston, Bachman-Turner Overdrive, Kansas, Styx, and Supertramp. Around and around they went, in constant rotation on the "mother of all playlists."

By choosing to ignore new wave and techno-pop bands (punk wasn't even considered), AOR programmers essentially entombed the music of the '70s. If you were listening to a station which played "classic rock" it meant you were listening to music created before the 1980s.

Just about everything associated with the '70s was considered "dinosaur rock." As if that wasn't enough, the dinosaurs were beginning to become extinct. The deaths of Elvis Presley in 1977, Keith Moon in 1978, John Bonham in 1979, John Lennon in 1980, and Bob Marley in 1981, left the music world without some of its most distinctive bands and stars.

There were a few standard bearers left standing. When John Travolta—the icon of 1970s style—donned cowboy boots and a pair of blue jeans for his role in the 1980 movie *Urban Cowboy* it was an unmistakable sign of just how different the climate of 1980s was going to be.

The sense of anxiety which accompanied these changes was captured with eloquent urgency by David Byrne of the Talking Heads on their 1979 hit "Life During Wartime."

*Talking Heads*

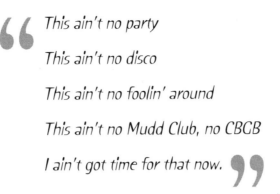

*This ain't no party*

*This ain't no disco*

*This ain't no foolin' around*

*This ain't no Mudd Club, no CBCB*

*I ain't got time for that now.*

Byrne had it right. There was a war going on, a cultural war which swept Ronald Reagan into office in 1980. The conservative agenda of the Reagan revolution was widely viewed, at the time, as a repudiation of the wild, anything-goes spirit of the "me decade." The 1980s would be known by an equally telling catch phrase: "Just say no."

There was a changing of the guard. The so-called moral majority viewed the unabashed hedonism of the '70s as the principal reason for the country's problems and consciously set about to re-instill a sense of family values. This included the efforts of Tipper Gore's Parents Music Research Center (PMRC), which held highly publicized Congressional hearings to investigate the content of rock lyrics.

Their efforts, which resulted in record labeling, sent a chilling message to musicians. If you were going to sing "getting high all the time, hope that you are, too," as Rick Derringer had on "Rock 'n' Roll, Hoochie Koo" or "she never lost her head even as she was giving head" as Lou Reed had on "Walk on the Wild Side" you were inviting a label warning for parents to monitor their children's listening habits.

The censorial urges of the 1980s were perhaps the most obvious example of how much things had changed since the sensation-seeking days of sex, drugs, and rock 'n' roll. But those days were numbered. The sexual revolution had been crushed by AIDS. Drugs were being condemned by the higher authorities. And rock 'n' roll had moved into the brave new world of synthesizers.

The party was over. The '70s were over. And, for a time, the whole era just seemed to disappear. It was the decade that time forgot, an aberration, a woozy, indulgent era where people had done crazy, inexplicable things. But it was no longer even a topic of conversation or debate. If anybody looked back during the '80s, it was usually to the '60s, not the '70s.

In terms of cultural interest, the '70s just ceased to be. Instead of a freewheeling party, people remembered scenes of burned-out helicopters in Iran, piles of bodies in Guyana, and Nixon resigning in disgrace—not exactly the kind of images which inspired the warm and fuzzy glow of nostalgia.

Did anyone miss the '70s in the '80s? Judging from the prices of memorabilia, the answer was no. Lunch boxes with David Cassidy's picture, Leif Garrett charm bracelets, Bay City Rollers thermoses, Farrah Fawcett posters—all of them could be bought in thrift stores and yard sales for mere pennies.

Why were the memories of the '70s so devalued? Had it been that bad? Or was this just a temporary lull of interest before a full-scale revival could bloom? With a little perspective, an answer was bound to reveal itself. As a loose rule, cycles of nostalgia operated in twenty-year loops, which meant the '70s were due to be resurrected sometime around 1990. And, true to form, that was the year everything changed.

A new decade—the 1990s—meant a new attitude about the 1970s. In typical '70s fashion, one '90s song, "Groove is in the Heart," managed to capture the moment. The sound of the song and the image of Deee-Lite, the group which sang it, represented something fresh and exciting. The song not only had heart, as the title suggested, but it had a whimsical, positive message. Even the band's name had a cheerful ring to it.

There was something different, yet strangely familiar, about Deee-Lite. Perhaps it was the fashion choices of lead singer Miss Lady Keir, decked out in platform shoes and various colorfully patterned synthetic-looking outfits in the video of "Groove is in the Heart." Or maybe it was the cameo appearance of Bootsy Collins, the outrageous

*Deee-lite*

funk star and erstwhile member of Parliament/Funkadelic. But both the video and the song were undeniably and distinctly '70s in flavor.

Soon after Deee-Lite surfaced, the infectiousness of '70s styles and sounds began to spread. At first, there was a trickle of interest in fashion circles and the underground music scene. And then suddenly, seemingly overnight, each and every one of the significant cultural icons of the '70s were back. Not only back, but back with a vengeance. John Travolta was back. Platform shoes were back. Bell-bottom pants were back. Lava lamps were back. Pot-smoking was back. Nixon was back. The smiley face was back. *Danny Bonaduce* was back.

Pundits began to search for the meaning of it all. They wondered whether the resurgence of interest in the '70s was just a phase, a temporary backlash against all those

*Nixon—he's tanned, he's rested, he's back.*

self-appointed moral leaders preaching about family values. Was the public sick of just saying no? And were they turning back to a time when everybody just said yes?

There could be no definitive explanation. Suddenly, for some reason, the '70s just felt right. All of the eccentricities, which once seemed threatening or annoying, now seemed harmless, even enviable, especially in a time of AIDS and crack cocaine. The idea of returning to the days when everybody wasn't so self-conscious and judgmental seemed more appealing than previously imaginable.

For many people the revival of the '70s had begun in earnest when "The Brady Bunch" turned up as a play, then a movie, then a slew of books. The meaning of the

"The Brady Bunch": *before and after*

Brady revival was much discussed in the media. Some dismissed it as just another regurgitation of trash culture. Others looked for hidden meanings: the semiotics of Jan Brady's sibling rivalry with Marcia, the long-lasting effects of divorce culture as portrayed on TV sitcoms, the androgyny of Alice the housekeeper.

At first blush, most people were satisfied to chalk the whole thing down to a bad case of nostalgia. But those who predicted the novelty of the '70s revival would wear off in one or two years were proven terribly short-sighted. If that hadn't been obvious before, it became a foregone conclusion when "Don't Stop," an upbeat Fleetwood Mac hit from the '70s, became the official campaign theme for Bill Clinton's 1992 presidential bid.

Clinton's choice of campaign theme songs proved, once and for all, just how powerful our memories of the '70s were and how important a role music played in evoking an image of better times. Suddenly, the music of the 1970s seemed uplifting and, even more surprising, relevant. An utterly banal party anthem like "Y.M.C.A."—which at the time seemed frothy to the point of obliviousness—became evocative of the less-complicated pleasures of the past. And, after Freddy Mercury's death, Queen's "Bohemian Rhapsody" became a poignant reminder of loss in the era of AIDS.

The once-derided, often-ridiculed, maligned sounds of the '70s became the hippest thing going. When "Stuck in the Middle With You," a hit for Stealers Wheel from 1973, was used by director Quentin Tarantino as a perversely-upbeat counterpoint to the gruesome ear-cutting scene in his cult film *Reservoir Dogs*, a full-blown revival of the music of the '70s seemed imminent.

Thanks to Tarantino—who resurrected the dormant career of John Travolta in his follow-up hit *Pulp Fiction*—almost every soundtrack had to feature at least one '70s classic.

"Bohemian Rhapsody" made a memorable appearance in *Wayne's World* as did Gary
Wright's "Dream Weaver," which also did double duty by appearing in *The People v.
Larry Flynt*. The Knack enjoyed a brief comeback thanks to the appearance of "My
Sharona" in *Reality Bites*. Lou Reed's "Perfect Day" and Iggy Pop's "Lust for Life"
added flavor to the drug-oriented *Trainspotting*. And lovable pop oddities like
Norman Greenbaum's "Spirit in the Sky" showed up in Ron Howard's *Apollo 13*.

At this point, it should have been clear to even the dimmest observer of trends
in popular culture that the sound of the '70s was back with a brand new reputation.
A virtual motherlode of cover versions began to blanket the airwaves. Mariah Carey's
"I'll Be There" (The Jackson Five) and "Without You" (Harry Nilsson); the Fugees
covered "Killing Me Softly With His Song" (Roberta Flack); Seal covered "Fly Like An
Eagle" (Steve Miller); Celine Dion covered "All by Myself" (Eric Carmen); Guns 'n'
Roses covered "Live and Let Die" (Paul McCartney and Wings); John Mellencamp

and Me'Shell Ndegeocello covered "Wild Night" (Van Morrison); the Cardigans sang "Sabbath Bloody Sabbath" (Black Sabbath); Tesla covered "Signs" (Five Man Electrical Band); Ice-Cube covered "One Nation Under a Groove" (Funkadelic); Gloria Estefan covered "Turn the Beat Around" (Vickie Sue Robinson); Sheryl Crow covered "D'Yer Maker" (Led Zeppelin); and the artist formerly known as Prince covered "Betcha By Golly, Wow" (Stylistics).

Peter Frampton's "Baby, I Love Your Way" was re-made into a bubbly pop reggae song by an anonymous group of studio musicians called Will to Power. When their cover version soared all the way to the top position on the Hot 100 *Billboard* pop single charts the coronation was complete: the '70s were king. Its caché was undeniable. Everybody wanted to be associated with the '70s. Performers were flaunting whatever connection they could claim. Garth Brooks fawned over James Taylor; Whitney Houston trotted out Chaka Khan; and George Michael not only dueted with Elton John on "Don't Let the Sun Go Down On Me" but joined the Mercury-less members of Queen onstage for a rendition of "Somebody to Love."

Part of the revival of the '70s was homage. Part of it was outright theft. Rap stars raided the vaults for samples of George Clinton and James Brown. Green Day stole the punk thunder of early Clash and early Jam. And practically every alternative rocker borrowed at least a few tricks and licks from '70s stalwarts like Neil Young and Led Zeppelin. It was "milking the K-tel" as Beck put it in the liner notes to his album *Mellow Gold*. A couple of extra tattoos and skin piercings and Alice Cooper became Marilyn Manson. A dash of the Jackson Five added to the wholesome looks of the Osmonds and—presto!—it was Hanson.

All of this activity represented a stunning turn of fortunes for the sound of the '70s. From a complete renunciation and banishment from the pop culture land-

scape to being embraced as one of the greatest eras of invention and inspiration in music, the revival of the '70s had undergone a series of unlikely twists and curious turns.

The most unusual turnabout may have been the stunning success in 1996 of Kiss, a band which everyone assumed was long past its prime. Kiss had always been one of the most critically reviled bands in rock history. During a particularly fallow period in the mid-1980s, the group had decided to take off their makeup and reveal their true identities. Big mistake. Kiss fans were not interested in the real identities of the group's members—they enjoyed the fantasy, the fireworks, and the four different cartoon character roles which each of the band's members played.

So in 1996 the members of Kiss made a shrewd move—they decided to put their makeup back on. Suddenly the band was playing to standing-room-only audiences. And by the end of the year, when all the gate receipts and sales from merchandise were counted up, it was duly noted by the rock press that the reunited members of Kiss had mounted the most lucrative rock tour of the year.

What explained their commercial triumph? Was it just another example of the public's insatiable appetite for every bit of cultural ephemera connected to the 1970s? Or was something else going on?

Another similar but unexplainable phenomenon occurred during time-outs at sporting events when "Y.M.C.A." by the Village People inspired cheerfully exhibitionistic participation rituals. All over the world, people stood up and voluntarily spelled out the letters of the late '70s hit and, from outward appearances, they seemed to be having a ball doing it. Was this nostalgia for disco? If so, then what happened to all of those people who were screaming "disco sucks" only ten years earlier? How many of them were now joining in on the fun?

*The Village People*

The immense success of Kiss and the nature of the "Y.M.C.A." phenomenon posed a series of intriguing questions about the '70s revival. What did it say about the needs and desires of the 1990s? Or, conversely, was it possible it didn't mean anything at all?

Some observers felt the latter was true. They prematurely concluded the revival was nothing more than kitsch and camp, that people were listening to the music of the '70s because it was so bad it was good. Like Kiss putting on its makeup, it was all a sham—an enjoyable sham, but a sham nonetheless.

But that explanation was too simple. First of all, the revival of the '70s showed no signs of going away, so it was not nearly as ephemeral as some supposed. It had simply gone too far to be just a kitschy and campy joke. Secondly, and perhaps more importantly, this explanation did not take into account all of the changes which had occurred in music since the 1970s. Analog had become digital. Vinyl albums had become compact discs. Live performances had turned into video clips.

The implication of these technological changes offered a more compelling reason for why the '70s revival was so different from previous cycles of nostalgia. In this digital age, the sources of our memories were subject to manipulation. Therefore, the nature of nostalgia, itself, was being called into question.

Perhaps people didn't really miss the era at all, they were merely sampling from the available images and sounds of the '70s. In other words, instead of engaging in indiscriminate forms of rose-colored nostalgia, they were deliberately choosing to reexperience the elements from the past which seemed to be worth another look or listen.

This fact was vividly demonstrated by the phenomenal success of *Star Wars*. Re-released in 1997, the twenty-year-old space epic outdrew all of its competition at the box-office. Shortly thereafter, the other installments of the trilogy, *The Empire Strikes Back* and *The Return of the Jedi* matched this feat. The bean counters marveled, "A bunch of old films were the top box-office attractions in the country. How could this be?"

The reason was simple: the movie-going public obviously preferred to re-experience some of their favorite movies from the past rather than see some new ones. And, yet, there was an extra added element to the renewed popularity of *Star Wars* which was symbolic of the revival of the '70s as a whole—it was not the original version which was sparking the sudden resurgence, it was a "new and improved" version.

In a widely publicized move, George Lucas, the director and producer of the films, had gone back into the studio to touch up the space epics, superimposing new special effects and even altering a few of the original scenes. Thanks to digital imaging that Lucas helped pioneer, the film had been "improved" by its creator, despite the fact the public had been perfectly content with the original product.

Like the *Star Wars* release, the Kiss reunion, and the Village People audience participation ritual, the revival of the '70s was an alluring simulation of the real thing, ahistorical in context and, thus, subject to new interpretations. This was

retrospective history as never witnessed before. The wonders of digital technology allowed artists as well as consumers to bring back the '70s they wanted to see and experience and, as usual, given the choice, people had made their decision—they wanted a better looking past.

The Elvis stamp vote of 1991 had proven that. It may have been the only time in recent memory that an icon of the '70s was publicly rejected. And, yet, in its own quirky way, the public's preference for the slender, ageless, primal Elvis over the puffy bloated Elvis of the '70s was a telling reflection on the nature of nostalgia. People tend to gravitate to an idealized past.

The desire to go back and improve the past is one of the defining characteristics of the '70s revival. The digital revolution has allowed recording artists in the '90s the opportunity to return to their original masters, correct the "mistakes," and to offer a new and improved '70s, the one that consumers apparently demand.

With digital imaging and sound manipulation reaching new levels of sophistication, the past has become a set of variables which are easily transformed into new entities. An emblematic example was Iggy Pop's decision in 1996 to fix the infamously botched mix of *Raw Power*. Although it received much less fanfare than the re-release of the *Star Wars* trilogy, Pop's decision to go back and tinker with the classic 1973 Stooges album had as many implications, in the realm of music, as Lucas' decision had in the realm of film.

In its original form, *Raw Power* had delivered just what it promised—an uncompromising, albeit violent, expression of everything which made rock music vital: slashing guitars, thunderous power chords, and the malignant charm of Iggy and the Stooges. So the question was: why was it necessary to go back and remix something which was already so perfectly flawed?

\* \* \* \* \* \* \*

*"The imperfection is what I love. When it comes to rock 'n' roll or whatever genre rock, whether it's jazz, blues, punk—it's the imperfection which I can relate to. That's what got me into music in the first place . . . when people try to perfect things that's when they blow it."*

—Joey Ramone on remixing old records, interview with author, 1997

\* \* \* \* \* \* \*

Although hailed as a masterpiece, over the years *Raw Power* had developed a reputation as a great record which suffered from bad sound. On some tracks, the drums were barely audible, on others, the vocals were obscured. Yet, despite these deficiencies, *Raw Power* was still considered one of the great rock 'n' roll records ever made. But when Pop decided to put his stamp of approval on the project, the unthinkable became official: the remixing would begin.

Suddenly, the lyrics of the album's opening track, "Search and Destroy," seemed prophetic:

*Look out honey*

*Cause I'm using technology*

*Ain't got time*

*To make no apologies.*

Pop offered no apologies. However, in the liner notes which accompanied the reissued and remixed *Raw Power*, he did reveal some ambivalence about getting involved with the project. Until it became abundantly clear that the record company would proceed without him, he had been non-committal about lending a hand. Even then, Pop confessed, he only agreed to participate because he understood the implications of his efforts. The newly-remixed *Raw Power* would, in his words, "become the version that people know." In other words, the old version—the original version—would cease to be widely distributed and the new version would become the new standard.

Which was better—the new or old *Raw Power*? As long as the old version remained available to listeners, they could make their own judgment. But should the original disappear, then the implications were enormous. How would any recording artist, in the future, know whether a creation was finished or still open to reinterpretation?

The technical ability to reshape and manipulate the collective memory through a computer chip has slowly but surely begun to change the nature of nostalgia. When is the past really past if it can be updated and changed at the slightest whim? By blurring the nature of what is original, no one can be sure. Moreover, if the revival of the '70s has proven anything, it is this: authenticity has very little to do with the reemergence of cultural icons.

Kiss is a perfect example. By re-applying their makeup and dusting off their old pyrotechnics in 1996, Kiss were, in essence, staging a simulation of a Kiss concert circa 1976. Underneath their familiar makeup, rock audiences couldn't see the wrinkles or the gray in their hair. It was like the group had never gone away.

And, in a sense, they never had. Even when the cultural icons of the '70s seemed to disappear in the 1980s, they had always existed as indelible images and sound. And now, in the 1990s, they were being brought back in new and improved ways. The

'70s in the '90s looked better than ever. They sounded better than ever. Even Richard Nixon—the most reviled and disgraced figure of the 1970s—was rehabilitated and restored to grandeur.

But do we really miss the '70s? Are we really nostalgic for waiting on line at the gas station? Or is something else going on? Could it be that the very nature of nostalgia is undergoing a radical change? Nostalgia used to be defined as "a longing for things, persons, or situations that are not present." But in a digital age, when information exists in a code that can be duplicated time after time with no diminution or loss of image, everything is up for grabs, pun intended.

How can we miss something that still exists? In a culture which seems bent on duplicating itself over and over again, the impermanence of video tape, digitization, and cyberspace ensures a never-ending flood of images from our past continuously reshaped until they seem fit for our re-consumption.

Thus our desire for something new and original has changed. Take, for example, the continuing popularity of *Grease*. According to *Billboard* magazine, the soundtrack to the 1978 musical starring John Travolta and Olivia Newton-John is selling more copies in the 1990s than it did in the 1970s. What explains this phenomenon? Nothing has changed about *Grease*.

The same question could be asked about Bob Marley. *Legends*, a compilation of Marley's greatest hits, continues to sell far more units in the 1990s than any album the reggae star released when he was alive. With no exaggeration, you could say Marley in death is bigger than life. And so, too, are the '70s. As time goes on, it is becoming apparent that this revival is really a continuation. The '70s never really went away. And now the decade shows no sign of disappearing.

Maybe we should take a moment before we sing the praises of the bean bag and blow-dryer years to consider the real decade, the real events, the real emotions. Context often gets lost in the wash of memories. Even back in the 1970s, when "Happy Days" was supposed to evoke the 1950s and *Beatlemania* was supposed to evoke the 1960s, we found out they could only replicate the feeling of the past, not resurrect the past itself.

The question of authenticity is a lot like the emotional allegiances over which is better—a vinyl album or a compact disc. A vinyl album is quirky and imperfect. But, once damaged, it forms its own personality. Little pops and scratches become a part of its character. Compact discs will not change. Thus, your attachment does not grow. What you put in is what you get out.

Taking the analogy to its logical conclusion, the perceived differences between the real '70s and the one we have brought back in the 1990s is not unlike the opposing forces between vinyl and CDs. One is an authentic expression, imperfect but personable. The other is a technological achievement and something to marvel at.

As impressive as the technological revival of the '70s has been, however, there will always be certain aspects of the past which can't be experienced through the wonders of technology. Take, for example, "The Six Million Dollar Man", that quintessentially hokey TV series starring Lee Majors as the Bionic Man, where the special effects were so antiquated that the superhero was always depicted as running and leaping in slow motion.

Thanks to the stunning leap of digital imaging, viewers will never be able to match the frustration with the deficiencies of the Bionic Man but, in a strange way, they may miss half the fun, which was imitating those deficiencies. The Bionic Man's superpowers were so unconvincing that hundreds of thousands of

*Ch-ch-ch-ch-ch-ch-ch-ch-ch-ch-ch.*

pre-adolescent boys and girls ran around in slow motion, affecting the "ch-ch-ch-ch" sound which was always heard in the background.

Certain aspects of the 1970s will never return. Other aspects will be resurrected but will be altered beyond recognition. However, for now, the revival of the '70s is nearly complete—almost everything about the decade had been exhumed and re-examined. Of course, Neil Diamond and Barbra Streisand haven't reunited to sing "You Don't Bring Me Flowers" . . . yet. And Eve Plumb refused to play Jan again in "The Brady Bunch Hour."

Otherwise, the process of restoring the '70s to its rightful place in the hallowed halls of ever-lasting cultural ephemera is nearing completion. Do we really miss the '70s? Let's put it this way: do you miss getting up from the couch to change the channel on your TV set? Didn't think so. But those who grew up in the '70s can take heart knowing that a decade that once seemed beyond redemption, let alone nostalgia, had now been thoroughly revived and enjoyed. All is forgiven.

Perhaps the newly enlightened attitude towards the '70s is best summed up by an old cliché: "Have a nice day" was a salutation, a safe and innocuous way of saying "You go your way, I'll go mine." In practical terms, it meant that you didn't have to love your neighbor but you could still muster up enough enthusiasm to wish them a nice day.

It is easy to see why those days seem so enviable. Before V-chips, before "Just Say No," before record labeling, before AIDS, before computer viruses, before "the Club," there was a brief moment in time when things weren't so terribly self-conscious. The '70s were, in fact, terribly *un*-self-conscious. You could strip off your clothes and streak, you could wear a perfectly absurd pair of pants, you could gyrate ridiculously on the disco dance floor . . . all without shame and embarrassment.

And in the future, whenever we are looking for a source of inspiration, imagination, ebullience, good humor, and great music, we'll know exactly where to go: back to the '70s.

# RHINO'S "ONLY IN THE '70s" TRIVIA QUIZ

1. In the early 1970s, three-fifths of the Turtles found themselves playing in what band?

2. Name Elvis Costello's career back-up band.

3. Name the three members of Lynyrd Skynyrd who died in a plane crash.

4. Name the article of clothing that was packaged in the original release of Alice Cooper's *School's Out*.

5. Name the artist who achieved notoriety for a stage act that included cutting his chest with glass.

6. Name the drummer who replaced Keith Moon in the Who.

7. Name the feature film that starred the Ramones.

8. Name the first rap record that achieved widespread popularity.

9. Name the first male rock star to seriously wear a dress on an album cover.

10. Name the performer who met with President Nixon and offered his services to be a narcotics agent.

11. Name the record company honcho who lost his job when it was discovered that he charged the cost of his son's Bar Mitzvah to his expense account.

12. Name the recording artist who called himself "The Night Tripper."

13. Name the respected drummer who hacked up and killed his mom.

14. Name the Rolling Stones guitarist chronologically between Brian Jones and Ron Wood.

15. Name the title of the 1974 album Paul McCartney wrote and produced for his brother.

16. The feature film *The Rose*, starring Bette Midler, was a thinly veiled depiction of what singer's life?

17. The notoriously unmusical Sid Vicious replaced whom in the Sex Pistols?

18. The Talking Heads' "Take Me to the River" was originally a hit for whom?

19. Who is known as the "Motor City Madman"?

20. Who was the Rolling Stones' "Angie" written about?

21. Name the rock group that wanted to title their live album *Skull Fuck*.

22. Name the rock star who relieved himself in an elevator as it made its way down to a crowded lobby.

23. Who wrote the original script to the Sex Pistols' feature film, *Who Killed Bambi?*

24. Name the record label owned by the Moody Blues.

25. Name the rocker who once ate five ice cream sundaes for breakfast and then passed out.

26. Salvador Dali created the first 360 degree holograph, using which rock artist as the subject?

27. Steely Dan was the name of what in the William Burrough's novel *Naked Lunch?*

28. What glitter era chartmaker performed as the high priest in the original *Jesus Christ Superstar* album?

29. What is Joey Ramone's real name?

30. What band which had dissolved were encouraged to reunite when David Bowie volunteered to produce and write their next single?

31. What rock group had to replace its lead singer when he was discovered dead from choking on his own vomit?

32 What was the name of the rock group Bruce Springsteen formed in college?

33. How did Mama Cass of the Mamas and the Papas really die?

34. Led Zeppelin's "Whole Lotta Love" borrowed heavily from a song titled "You Need Lovin'" originally written and performed by whom?

35. Little Roger & the Goosebumps took some heat when they combined the lyrics of "Gilligan's Isle" with what song?

36. Name rock's most famous former grave digger.

37. Name the 1970s hit that was the most apparent expression of marijuana use.

38. Name the first member of the Eagles to leave the group.

39. Name the hit group whose two most prominent members committed suicide.

40. Name the notoriously titled "B" side of Patti Smith's pre-Arista, privately printed single.

41. Name the record company that briefly used the promotional phrase "Even our socks smell of success."

42. About whom did Bob Dylan write "Joey"?

43. About whom did Joni Mitchell write "A Free Man in Paris"?

44. Although people commonly site Eric Clapton, Jeff Beck, and Jimmy Page as the Yardbirds most prominent ex-members, name the group's other commercially successful alumnus.

45. Although the Village People's records made much use of studio singers, name the group's lead singer who sang on most of their hits.

46. Early in his career, Billy Idol hit the charts as a member of what band?

47. Due to the Sex Pistols' raucus post-signing celebration at their offices, which label subsequently released the band from their new contract?

48. Eric Clapton's unrequited love for whom inspired him to write the *Layla* album.

# Answers

(Just in case you wanted to confirm all that you already know.)

1. The Mothers of Invention
2. The Attractions
3. Ronnie Van Zandt, Steve & Cassie Gaines
4. Underpants
5. Iggy Pop
6. Kenny Jones
7. *Rock 'n' Roll High School*
8. "Rapper's Delight" by the Sugarhill Gang
9. David Bowie, on the English release of *The Man Who Sold the World.*
10. Elvis Presley
11. Clive Davis
12. Dr. John (a.k.a. Mac Rebeneck)
13. Jim Gordon
14. Mick Taylor
15. *McGear*
16. Janis Joplin
17. Glen Matlock, who was kicked out for liking the Beatles
18. Al Green
19. Ted Nugent
20. David Bowie's wife, Angela
21. Grateful Dead
22. Ozzy Osbourne
23. Roger Ebert
24. Threshold
25. Elvis Presley
26. Alice Cooper
27. A dildo
28. Paul Raven a.k.a. Gary Glitter
29. Jeffrey Hyman
30. Mott the Hoople
31. Bon Scott of AC/DC
32. Steel Mill
33. From a heart attack, not from choking on a ham sandwich as was rumored.
34. Muddy Waters
35. "Stairway to Heaven"
36. Rod Stewart
37. "One Toke Over the Line" by Brewer & Shipley
38. Bernie Leadon, after the fourth album
39. Badfinger
40. "Piss Factory"
41. Stiff Records
42. Gangster Joey Gallo
43. David Geffen
44. Bassist Paul Samwell-Smith who produced Cat Stevens, Carly Simon, and Jethro Tull, among others
45. Victor Willis
46. Generation X
47. A & M Records
48. George Harrison's wife, Patti Harrison

# RHINO'S '70s DISCOGRAPHY

## Significant Sounds of the '70s

## A

| | | |
|---|---|---|
| ABBA | ABBA | 1975 |
| AC/DC | Highway to Hell | 1979 |
| Aerosmith | Rocks | 1976 |
| Aerosmith | Toys in the Attic | 1975 |
| The Allman Brothers | At the Filmore East | 1971 |
| The Allman Brothers | Eat a Peach | 1972 |
| The Allman Brothers | Brothers and Sisters | 1973 |
| America | America | 1972 |

| | | |
|---|---|---|
| Argent | Argent | 1970 |
| Average White Band | Average White Band | 1974 |

## B

| | | |
|---|---|---|
| B-52s | B-52s | 1979 |
| Bachman-Turner Overdrive | Best of B.T.O. (So Far) | 1974 |
| Bad Company | Bad Company | 1974 |
| Badfinger | No Dice | 1971 |
| Bay City Rollers | Greatest Hits | 1977 |
| Bee Gees | Bee Gees Gold, Vol. 1 | 1976 |
| Bee Gees | Saturday Night Fever | 1977 |
| Big Star | Radio City | 1972 |
| Black Sabbath | Paranoid | 1971 |
| Bobbie Bland | Dreamer | 1974 |
| Blondie | Parallel Lines | 1978 |
| Blue Oyster Cult | Agents of Fortune | 1976 |
| Boomtown Rats | A Tonic For the Troops | 1979 |
| Boston | Boston | 1976 |
| David Bowie | Rise & Fall of Ziggy Stardust | 1972 |
| Bread | Baby, I'm-A Want You | 1972 |
| James Brown | The Payback | 1974 |
| Jackson Browne | Late For the Sky | 1974 |

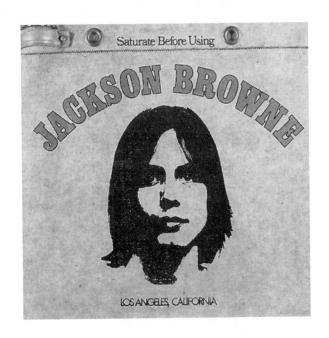

Saturate Before Using

JACKSON BROWNE

LOS ANGELES, CALIFORNIA

| | | |
|---|---|---|
| Jackson Browne | Running On Empty | **1977** |
| Jimmy Buffett | Changes In Attitudes, Changes in Lattitudes | 1977 |

𝒞

| | | |
|---|---|---|
| Can | Flow Motion | 1976 |
| Carpenters | Singles (1969-1973) | 1973 |
| The Cars | The Cars | 1978 |
| Harry Chapin | Short Stories | 1974 |
| Cheap Trick | Heaven Tonight | 1978 |

| | | |
|---|---|---|
| Cheap Trick | Live at Budokan | 1979 |
| Chic | C'est Chic | 1978 |
| Chicago | Greatest Hits | 1975 |
| Eric Clapton | 461 Ocean Boulevard | 1974 |
| Clash | Clash | 1977 |
| **Clash** | **London Calling** | **1979** |
| Joe Cocker | I Can Stand A Little Rain | 1974 |
| Commodores | Natural High | 1978 |
| Alice Cooper | Greatest Hits | 1974 |
| Elvis Costello | Armed Forces | 1979 |
| Elvis Costello | This Year's Model | 1978 |

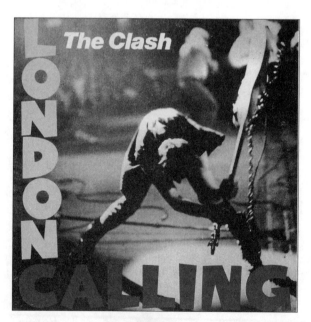

The RHINO History of Rock 'n' Roll

| | | |
|---|---|---|
| Elvis Costello | My Aim Is True | **1977** |
| Creedence Clearwater Revival | Chronicle | 1976 |
| Crosby, Stills, Nash & Young | Deja-vu | 1970 |
| Crosby, Stills & Nash | So Far | 1974 |

# 𝒟

| | | |
|---|---|---|
| Deep Purple | Machine Head | 1972 |
| John Denver | The Best of John Denver | 1974 |
| Derek & The Dominoes | Layla & Other Assorted Love Songs | 1970 |
| Devo | Q: Are We Not Men? | 1978 |
| | A: We Are Devo! | |

| Neil Diamond | His Twelve Greatest Hits | 1974 |
| The Doobie Brothers | Best of The Doobie Brothers | 1976 |
| Doors | L. A. Woman | 1971 |
| Dr. Feelgood | Malpractice | 1975 |
| Ducks Deluxe | Ducks Deluxe | 1974 |
| Bob Dylan | Blood on the Tracks | 1975 |

| Eagles | Their Greatest Hits(1971-1975) | 1976 |
| Eagles | Desperado | 1973 |
| Eagles | Hotel California | 1976 |
| Earth, Wind & Fire | Best of Earth, Wind & Fire, Vol. 1 | 1978 |
| Electric Light Orchestra | Greatest Hits | 1979 |
| Emerson, Lake & Palmer | Emerson, Lake & Palmer | 1971 |
| Brian Eno | Another Green World | 1975 |

| Faust | Faust | 1971 |
| Flamin' Groovies | Shake Some Action | 1976 |
| Fleetwood Mac | Fleetwood Mac | 1975 |
| Fleetwood Mac | Rumours | 1977 |

| Flo & Eddie | Illegal, Immoral, and Fattening | 1975 |
| Foghat | Foghat Live | 1977 |
| Foreigner | Foreigner | 1977 |
| Peter Frampton | Frampton Comes Alive! | 1976 |
| Funkedelic | Maggot Brain | 1971 |
| Funkedelic | One Nation Under a Groove | 1978 |

#

| Peter Gabriel | Peter Gabriel | 1977 |
| Marvin Gaye | Let's Get It On | 1973 |
| Marvin Gaye | What's Going On | 1971 |

| Genesis | Lamb Lies Down on Broadway | 1974 |
| Grateful Dead | American Beauty | 1970 |
| Grateful Dead | What a Long Strange Trip It's Been | 1977 |
| Grateful Dead | Workingman's Dead | 1970 |
| Al Green | Greatest Hits | 1975 |
| The Guess Who | The Best of The Guess Who | 1971 |

| George Harrison | All Things Must Pass | 1970 |
| Isaac Hayes | Shaft | 1971 |
| Heart | Dreamboat Annie | 1976 |
| Hot Chocolate | Cicero Park | 1974 |

## J

| Jackson 5 | Anthology | 1976 |
| Joe Jackson | Look Sharp | 1979 |
| Michael Jackson | Off the Wall | 1979 |
| Jam | All Mod Cons | 1978 |
| Jethro Tull | Aqualung | 1971 |
| Billy Joel | Piano Man | 1974 |

| | | |
|---|---|---|
| **Billy Joel** | **The Stranger** | **1977** |
| Elton John | Greatest Hits | 1974 |
| Elton John | Honky Chateau | 1972 |
| Elton John | Goodbye Yellow Brick Road | 1973 |
| Rickie Lee Jones | Rickie Lee Jones | 1979 |
| Janis Joplin | Pearl | 1971 |
| Joy Division | Unknown Pleasures | 1979 |

| | | |
|---|---|---|
| K. C. & The Sunshine Band | K. C. & The Sunshine Band | 1975 |

| | | |
|---|---|---|
| Carole King | Tapestry | 1971 |
| The Kinks | Muswell Hillbillies | 1971 |
| Kiss | Alive! | 1975 |
| Knack | The Knack | 1979 |
| Kool & the Gang | Spirit of the Boogie | 1975 |
| Kraftwerk | Autobahn | 1974 |

## *L*

| | | |
|---|---|---|
| Led Zeppelin | (IV) | 1971 |
| **Led Zeppelin** | **Physical Graffiti** | **1975** |
| John Lennon/Plastic Ono Band | | 1970 |
| John Lennon | Imagine | 1971 |
| Little Feat | Feats Don't Fail Me Now | 1974 |
| Loggins and Messina | Best of Friends | 1976 |
| Nick Lowe | Pure Pop for Now People | 1978 |
| Lynyrd Skynyrd | Pronounced Leh-Nerd Skin-Nerd | 1973 |
| Lynyrd Skynyrd | One More From the Road | 1976 |

## *M*

| | | |
|---|---|---|
| Bob Marley and the Wailers | Natty Dread | 1975 |
| Dave Mason | The Very Best of Dave Mason | 1978 |
| Curtis Mayfield | Curtis | 1970 |

| Curtis Mayfield | Superfly | 1972 |
| Paul McCartney and Wings | Band on the Run | 1973 |
| Paul McCartney and Wings | Wings Greatest | 1978 |
| Don McLean | American Pie | 1971 |
| **Meatloaf** | **Bat Out of Hell** | **1978** |
| The Steve Miller Band | The Joker | 1973 |
| The Steve Miller Band | Fly Like an Eagle | 1976 |
| Joni Mitchell | Blue | 1971 |
| Joni Mitchell | Court and Spark | 1974 |
| Modern Lovers | The Modern Lovers | 1976 |

| | | |
|---|---|---|
| Moody Blues | Seventh Sojourn | 1972 |
| Van Morrison | Moondance | 1970 |
| **Mott the Hoople** | **Greatest Hits** | **1975** |
| Move | Shazam | 1970 |

## 𝒩

| | | |
|---|---|---|
| New York Dolls | New York Dolls | 1973 |
| Randy Newman | Sail Away | 1972 |

## 𝒪

| | | |
|---|---|---|
| O'Jays | Back Stabbers | 1972 |

| Mike Oldfield | Tubular Bells | 1973 |

| Graham Parker | Howlin' Wind | 1976 |
| Graham Parker | Squeezing Out Sparks | 1979 |
| Parliament | Funkentelechy vs. the Placebo Syndrome | 1977 |
| Parliament | Mothership Connection | 1976 |
| The Alan Parsons Project | Tales of Mystery and Imagination | 1975 |
| Tom Petty and the Heartbreakers | Damn the Torpedoes | 1979 |
| Pink Floyd | Dark Side of the Moon | 1973 |

| | | |
|---|---|---|
| Pink Floyd | The Wall | 1979 |
| Police | Outlandos D'Amour | 1978 |
| Prince | Prince | 1979 |
| John Prine | John Prine | 1971 |
| Pure Prairie League | Bustin' Out | 1972 |

# Q

| | | |
|---|---|---|
| Queen | Night at the Opera | 1975 |

# R

| | | |
|---|---|---|
| Bonnie Raitt | Give It Up | 1972 |
| Ramones | Rocket to Russia | 1977 |
| Raspberries | Raspberries' Best Featuring Eric Carmen | 1976 |
| Lou Reed | Transformer | 1972 |
| Emitt Rhodes | Emitt Rhodes | 1970 |
| The Rolling Stones | Sticky Fingers | 1971 |
| The Rolling Stones | Exile On Main Street | 1972 |
| The Rolling Stones | Some Girls | 1978 |
| Linda Ronstadt | Heart Like a Wheel | 1974 |

The RHINO History of Rock 'n' Roll

| | | |
|---|---|---|
| Todd Rundgren | Runt | 1970 |
| Todd Rundgren | Something/Anything? | 1972 |
| Rutles | The Rutles | 1978 |

#

| | | |
|---|---|---|
| Santana | Santana III | 1971 |
| Bob Seger | Night Moves | 1976 |
| Bob Seger | Stranger in Town | 1978 |
| Sex Pistols | Never Mind the Bollocks | 1977 |
| Carly Simon | No Secrets | 1972 |
| Paul Simon | Paul Simon | 1972 |
| Simon & Garfunkel | Greatest Hits | 1972 |
| Simon & Garfunkel | Bridge Over Troubled Water | 1970 |
| Slade | Sladest | 1973 |
| Sly & the Family Stone | Greatest Hits | 1970 |
| Sly & The Family Stone | There's a Riot Goin' On | 1971 |
| Patti Smith | Horses | 1975 |
| Sparks | Kimono My House | 1974 |
| The Specials | The Specials | 1979 |
| Spirit | The Twelve Dreams of Dr. Sardonicus | 1970 |
| Bruce Springsteen | Born to Run | 1975 |
| Bruce Springsteen | Darkness on the Edge of Town | 1978 |

| | | |
|---|---|---|
| Bruce Springsteen | Born to Run | 1975 |
| Bruce Springsteen | Darkness on the Edge of Town | 1978 |
| Ringo Starr | Ringo | 1973 |
| Steely Dan | Countdown to Ecstasy | 1973 |
| Steely Dan | Pretzel Logic | 1974 |
| Steely Dan | Aja | 1977 |
| Cat Stevens | Tea for the Tillerman | 1970 |
| Rod Stewart | Never a Dull Moment | 1972 |
| Rod Stewart | Every Picture Tells a Story | 1971 |
| Stooges | Fun House | 1970 |
| Stooges | Raw Power | 1973 |

| Stylistics | The Stylistics | 1971 |
| Donna Summer | On the Radio (Greatest Hits) | 1979 |
| Supertramp | Breakfast in America | 1979 |
| Sweet | Desolation Boulevard | 1975 |

| Talking Heads | More Songs About Buildings & Food | 1978 |
| Talking Heads | Talking Heads '77 | 1977 |
| James Taylor | Sweet Baby James | 1970 |
| Television | Marquee Moon | 1977 |
| Traffic | John Barleycorn Must Die | 1970 |
| T. Rex | Electric Warrior | 1971 |

| Van Halen | Van Halen | 1978 |
| Velvet Underground | Loaded | 1970 |

| Tom Waits | Small Change | 1976 |
| War | Greatest Hits | 1976 |
| The Who | Who's Next | 1971 |

| | | |
|---|---|---|
| The Who | Meaty, Beaty, Big, and Bouncy | 1971 |
| The Who | Quadrophenia | 1973 |
| The Edgar Winter Group | Shock Treatment | 1974 |
| Stevie Wonder | Anthology | 1977 |
| Stevie Wonder | Innervisions | 1973 |
| Stevie Wonder | Songs In the Key of Life | 1976 |
| Stevie Wonder | Talking Book | 1972 |

| | | |
|---|---|---|
| Yes | The Yes Album | 1971 |
| Yes | Fragile | 1972 |
| Neil Young | Decade | 1977 |
| Neil Young | After The Gold Rush | 1970 |
| Neil Young | Harvest | 1972 |
| Neil Young | Rust Never Sleeps | 1979 |
| Frank Zappa | Apostrophe | 1974 |
| Misc. *The Harder They Come* | Original Soundtrack | 1972 |

# Resources

For hard-to-find groups like Faust, contact Cuneiform Records, P.O. Box 8427, Silver Springs, MD 20907 Fax: (301) 589-1819. Website: members.aol.com/Cuneiform2/cuneiform.html

For the sleazy side of the '70s contact Last Gasp of San Francisco, 777 Florida Street, San Francisco, CA 94110. Fax: (415) 824-1836. Website: www.lastgasp.com

For underground video and audio from the '70s, try the website of Duane Dimock: www.duanedimock.com

For original '70s mechandise contact: Love Saves the Day, 119 Second Avenue, New York, NY 10003 Phone: (212)228-3802

For everything you need to know about 8-Tracks, try the website 8-Track Mind: www.hickory.net/malco/8track

For record reviews of the '70s best-selling albums, try the Super Seventies Rocksite! at www.geocities.com/sunsetstrip/8678/index.html

For more information about getting your hands on the music described herein, either call Rhino Records at (800) 432-0020 or check out their website at www.rhino.com.

# *Photo Credits*

CHAPTER 1: HAPPY DAYS

© 1997 AP World Wide Photos—6, 18. © 1997 Archive Photos—2, 13. © 1997 UPI Corbis-Bettman—7, 9, 11, 15. © 1997 Gerald Ford Library—14.

CHAPTER 2: GIMME GIMME SHOCK ROCK

© 1997 AP World Wide Photos—24, 32, 38. © 1997 Archive Photos—22, 27. © 1997 UPI Corbis-Bettman—37. © 1997 Faulty Products—42.

CHAPTER 3: THE REVOLUTION WILL NOT BE PLAYLISTED

© 1997 AP World Wide Photos—47, 49, 53, 55, 58. © 1997 Archive Photos—45, 56. © 1997 Berserkley—51.

CHAPTER 4: ONE NATION UNDER A GROOVE

© 1997 AP World Wide Photos—66, 69, 74. © 1997 Archive Photos—67, 72, 77, 78. © 1997 UPI Corbis-Bettman—83.

CHAPTER 5: IT CAME FROM THE '70S

© 1997 AP World Wide Photos—88, 91, 101. © 1997 Archive Photos—97, 103. © 1997 UPI Corbis-Bettman—92, 94. ©1993 Henry Diltz—90.

CHAPTER 6: FREEBIRD! WHIPPING POST! LAYLA! IT'S A ROCK-BLOCK WEEKEND!

©1997 AP World Wide Photos—120, 125, 127. ©1997 Archive Photos—113, 115, 118, 123.

CHAPTER 7: BAD GIRLS, GOOD TIMES, FREAK OUT!

© 1997 World Wide Photos—151. © 1997 Archive Photos—136, 139, 141, 154. © 1997 UPI Corbis-Bettman—145, 148.

CHAPTER 8: THE END OF THE '70S

© 1997 AP World Wide Photos—160, 165, 178. © 1997 Archive Photos—164, 167, 170.

DISCOGRAPHY

© 1997 Atlantic Recording Group—193, 197, 199. © 1997 Elektra Entertainment Group—189, 202. © 1997 Columbia Records—191, 195. ©1997 Epic Records—190, 198.

The **RHINO** History of Rock 'n' Roll

# About the Author

Eric Lefcowitz specializes in writing about pop culture. He has written several books including *The Monkees Tale* and *Tomorrow Never Knows: The Beatles Last Concert*. His articles have appeared in various publications, including *The New York Times*. He lives in New York City.

# About Rhino Records

In the 1970s music fans Richard Foos and Harold Bronson started the Rhino Records label out of the back of their record store, beginning with novelty records and then following a long path to become the premiere reissue label. Rhino Records' repackaging work has been acclaimed by *The L.A. Times*, *The New York Times*, *Rolling Stone*, and *Spin* magazine and has led to popular offshoots such as Kid Rhino; Word Beat, for poetry and spoken word; movie soundtracks released with Turner Entertainment; and the Atlantic Records jazz catalogue.

# Rhino History of Rock 'n' Roll: The '70s

## CD SONG LIST

1. ROUNDABOUT - Yes

2. DRAGGIN' THE LINE - Tommy James

3. HELLO HOORAY - Alice Cooper

4. RIGHT PLACE, WRONG TIME - Dr. John

5. UNDERCOVER ANGEL - Alan O'Day

6. GET DOWN TONIGHT - K.C. & The Sunshine Band

7. INTERVIEW WITH DON CORLEONE - National Lampoon (Chevy Chase, Billy Crystal, & Bill Murray)

8. INTERVIEW WITH ALI AND FOREMAN - National Lampoon (Chevy Chase, Billy Crystal, & Bill Murray)
Hear other great National Lampoon moments on
The Best Of National Lampoon Radio Hour (R2 72263)

*COMING IN 1998*

# Rhino History of Rock 'n' Roll: The '80s

FOR MORE LISTINGS OF BYRON PREISS MULTIMEDIA
PUBLICATIONS AND CD-ROMS,
EXPLORE OUR WEBSITE.

www.byronpreiss.com